Viv Peterson

happy birthday
A Guide To Special Parties For Children

Many "Happy Birthdays"!
from,
Susan and Melinda

Editor: Marilyn McFarlane
Cover design: Abigail Anstey
Back cover photograph: Steve Steckley
Left to right: Ashley King, Melinda King, Teresa Smith,
Brian Smith and Susan Smith

Published by White Pine Press
3 Hotspur, Lake Oswego, Oregon 97034

Copyright © 1983 by Susan Smith and Melinda King
All Rights Reserved
Printed in the United States of America
First Edition
Library of Congress Catalog Number 83-060669
ISBN 0-9610988-0-5

To Ashley, Brian, and Teresa

White Pine Press
Lake Oswego, Oregon

happy birthday
A Guide To Special Parties For Children

by Susan Smith
and Melinda King

Illustrated By
Loralee Newman

Table of Contents

Preface	
Creating A Special Party	

Party Plans	Page
Old MacDonald's Farm	1
Mother Goose	7
Fire Engine #9	13
Alphabet Fun	17
Sesame Street	21
Land of Make Believe	25
All Aboard	31
A Teddy Bears' Picnic	35
Tiaras and Tophats	39
Home On The Range	43
Wizard of Oz	49
Under The Big Top	55
Pirate Treasure	61
Making Miniatures	67
Rover, Come Over	73
Beyond The Stars	79
Bingo!	85
Bon Appetit	89
Globe Trotting	93
PJ Surprise	97
Knights & Dragons	101
Hobo Heaven	107
Play Ball!	111
Japanese Tea	117
Age of Aquarius	123

Games	129
Crafts	147
Birthday Symbols	155
Index	159

Preface

To create a special party for a child is to create a memory that lasts a lifetime. If it's a birthday party, it has an almost-magical significance. It can be simple, and it need not be costly, but a successful party does take planning. There's no greater reward than a hug from a satisfied child saying, "That was the best party I ever had!"

As mothers and teachers, we've organized dozens of children's events and have often been asked to suggest ideas that won't leave the house a wreck and the parent, usually the mother, in a state of exhaustion.

This book was written in sympathetic response to those requests. We believe your child's party should be a pleasant memory for you, too!

Some of the suggestions offered in *Happy Birthday* are more elaborate than others, and some take more time. Pick those that suit your taste, time and budget. Most are inexpensive and homemade, requiring only ingenuity, easily obtained materials, and planning.

Just don't get so caught up in organizing that you forget to sing "Happy Birthday" to the birthday child; it has happened! Enjoy yourself, and know that you are creating a once-in-a-lifetime occasion that will be a treasured memory for years to come.

Melinda and Susan

Creating A Special Party

PREPARATION

The key to a successful party is in the planning. Be sure you have all the materials together beforehand for each activity scheduled. The birthday child can help in a number of ways, making the party extra-special while encouraging responsibility and creativity. For example, a child would enjoy making the shoebox cages that hold the wild creatures captured in "Under The Big Top."

HELPERS

A friend, relative, or the birthday child's older brother or sister can be of invaluable assistance. The Wagonmaster in "Home On The Range" or Long John Silver in "Pirate Treasure" are perfect roles for helpers.

THEME

A theme provides a focus and makes your party special. It reflects the interests and age of the birthday child.

INVITATIONS

Artistic ability is not a requirement for designing your own invitations! Some of the most charming we've seen are simple pictures crayoned by the birthday child. Invitations should note that this is a *birthday* party, as well as stating clearly the child's name, address, phone number, and the party date. Include the party's beginning and ending times, and request a reply. For an invitation that is fun and different, try something unusual like the hardboiled egg in "Old MacDonald's Farm."

DECORATIONS

Make decorations to fit the theme. Decide before the party whether you will keep the decorations or send them home with guests as favors. If they are taken by guests, be sure you have enough for each person, including the birthday child.

GUESTS

Invite one guest for every year of the birthday child's age (an 8-year-old would invite eight guests). This handy rule provides a structure that lets everyone know what to expect from year to year.

PARTY AREA

Keep the party confined to one specific room or area. Offer plenty of space, but make the limits clear. Decorations can help — for example, the fairy footprints in "Land of Make Believe" lead guests to the party area.

ACTIVITIES

Alternate active games with quiet ones. Most of the activities listed in our parties follow this pattern. The party begins with an activity that can be played while waiting for everyone to arrive, and it ends with a calm, quiet activity while guests wait to be taken home. When planning the party, decide approximately how much time each activity will take. Have a few extra game ideas prepared in case they're needed.

PRIZES

Avoid prizes if possible. Cheer and clap for the winner instead.

FAVORS

Provide a basket or decorated paper bag for each child's favors and take-home items. Include the birthday child. Label the bag with the guest's name and keep it by the front door. Buy or make at least one extra favor to replace those lost, broken, or eaten by the dog. The following favor suggestions are inexpensive and popular:

- pocket games
- coloring and activity books
- card games
- marbles
- pressout books
- paint-with-water books
- records
- stickers
- guessing game books
- story books
- invisible ink books
- puzzles
- poster art
- puzzle art
- car cases for small cars
- snap-together model airplane and car kits

large and small balls
items personally decorated (use permanent marking pens) — T-shirts, hats, socks, ribbons, barrettes, cloth belts, shoelaces, pillow cases

GIFTS

Bringing gifts to the birthday child is a happy party tradition. Here are some suggestions to make the present-opening ceremony enjoyable for everyone:

- At a party for younger children, collect the birthday gifts as soon as the guests arrive and place them completely out of the way until they are opened at the end of the party.
- Have the birthday child give small favors (wrapped or unwrapped) to the guests at present-opening time so they, too, have "gifts."
- Have guests sit in a circle, each holding a present for the birthday child. One guest spins an empty soft drink bottle turned on its side. When the bottle stops, the person it points to hands a present to the birthday child. Continue until all presents are open.
- For inexpensive gift ideas, see Favors list.

REFRESHMENTS

Gear refreshments to the theme of the party, and keep them simple. This is not the time to try your new recipe for spinach quiche. Peanut butter and jelly, hot dogs, pizza, hamburgers, a special cake — these are the treats guaranteed to please. If you prepare a fancy cake, it's best to serve plain vanilla ice cream with it. When cutting a cake in a particular shape, first make a pattern on a paper napkin. Place the pattern on the cooled cake and cut around it. Serve small portions to young children, since they are too excited to eat much. For older children and teenagers, have plenty of extras. They can and will eat it all!

Old MacDonald's Farm

*"Here a chick, there a chick,
Everywhere a chick chick ..."*

INVITATIONS
- Buy seed packets, or save old ones. Write the invitation on the outside of the packet or, if it's empty, place the invitation inside the packet.
- Staple a small package of seeds to the inside of a folded card. Write "Old MacDonald had a farm — and on his farm he had a birthday party for Patrick. Please help celebrate in the barnyard at [address]."
- Copy a picture of an appealing animal or a barn from a baby animal book, and use it to draw invitations on colored construction paper.

- Color hardboiled eggs and write the invitations directly on the eggs with felt pen. Deliver to the guests' mailboxes or leave on their doorsteps.
- Suggest that guests wear "farmer clothes" — jeans, overalls, straw hats, bandanas, etc. Have extra items on hand.

DECORATIONS
- Play records of "Farmer in the Dell" and "Old MacDonald."
- Place farm items around the "barnyard." In the fall, use bales of hay (very messy), cornstalks, squash, gourds, and pumpkins.

In the spring, use watering cans, seed catalogs, and potted plants.
- Make a scarecrow by stuffing an old shirt and pair of pants with pillows or newspapers. Use a paper bag with a felt-penned face for the head, or push a rag doll into the neck of the shirt so the doll's head is the scarecrow's face. Top it with a straw hat and a crow cut from black paper, and lean it in the corner.

- Place a bale of hay in a red wagon.
- Place three or four small plastic farm animals to "graze" on each guest's colorful paper plate or on the middle of the table. The animals can be used as favors.
- Position stuffed animals behind a row of short wire garden fencing.
- Tape a farm scene mural to a wall. Draw the scene on butcher paper before the party.
- Place library books picturing farm animals on a low table, to keep early arrivals occupied.

ACTIVITIES
Planting Time
Each guest is given a paper cup, labeled with the child's name, and a few large seeds (such as nasturtium or bean). The cups have been half-filled with potting soil. The guests plant the seeds in their cups, and the parent or helper pours a few drops of water in each one. The cups are taken home as favors. Seeds will mature faster if they are soaked in water the night before the party.

Hayride
Each guest gets a turn riding in the "haywagon," pulled by the parent or helper. This is a good activity to do while waiting for everyone to finish planting seeds.

Fetch The Cows
This is the farmer's version of *Hide and Seek*. The farmer (It) pretends to be busy feeding the chickens while the cows (other players) hide. At the sound of a helper's rooster crow, the farmer must hunt for the stray cows, who moo from their hiding places until they are all found and brought back to the fence (a chalk mark or length of string). The first cow found becomes the next farmer.

Animal Charades
Players sit in a circle and sing "Old MacDonald" (words follow), but when they reach the name of an animal in the song, they take turns imitating its actions, instead of singing the word. The others guess what the animal is before continuing with the song.

"Old MacDonald"

Old MacDonald had a farm, E-I-E-I-O. And on his farm he had some chicks; E-I-E-I-O. With a chick chick here, and a chick chick there; here a chick, there a chick, everywhere a chick chick; Old MacDonald had a farm; E-I-E-I-O.

The list of animals and sounds grows longer as others are added each time the verse is sung.

    Ducks ... quack, quack
    Geese ... honk, honk
    Sheep ... baa, baa
    Hens ... cluck, cluck
    Cows ... moo, moo
    Horses ... neigh, neigh
    Donkeys ... hee haw, hee haw
    Pigs ... oink, oink

Old MacDonald March
   Guests play Musical Chairs (see Games, page 139) to the music of an "Old MacDonald" record.
Pin The Tail On The Donkey
   (See Games, page 134). For a change, try *Pin The Curly Tail On The Pig.*

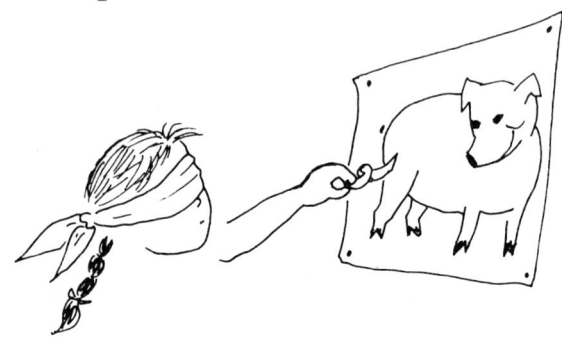

Animals Birthday
   (See Games, page 129.)
Corn Pictures
   Guests make pictures to take home by pasting popcorn kernels, dried peas, and beans on construction paper.
Harvest Time
   Guests harvest their own lunches by gathering them from shrubs in the yard. The lunches are easy-to-pack foods in sealed plastic bags: small sandwiches, carrot sticks, apple wedges, etc.
Farmer In The Dell
   Players join hands in a circle, with one person in the middle as the Farmer. As they walk, singing "Farmer In The Dell," the Farmer picks a Wife, who joins him in the middle. This continues in the order given below, until all the children have been chosen.

Farmer In The Dell

The farmer in the dell, The farmer in the dell; Hi-ho, the derry-o, The farmer in the dell. The farmer takes a wife ... The wife takes a child ... The child takes a nurse ... The nurse takes a dog ... The dog takes a cat ... The cat takes a rat ... The rat takes a cheese ... The cheese stands alone.

In The Barnyard
If a toy that makes farm noises is available, the guests sit in a circle on the floor. While the birthday child pulls the cord on the toy, they guess which animal is making the sound.

For a party away from home, some zoos have barnyard areas where visitors may touch and watch the animals — a great treat for preschoolers.

REFRESHMENTS
- Garden treats such as corn on the cob, cut in small pieces; raw vegetables (carrots, celery, fresh peas); hardboiled eggs, decorated by the birthday child with colored felt pens; watermelon pieces
- Harvest Bowl (recipe follows)
- Scarecrow Shake (recipe follows)
- Bagged lunches (see *Harvest Time* activity)

Cake
- Barnyard sheet cake. Arrange small plastic or cardboard cut-out animals inside a toothpick fence; place a toy barn and silo nearby. Mound yellow coconut for haystacks and put a tiny bucket (thimble or toothpaste cap) containing a drop of milk under the cow.
- Animal cake. Shape a cake into the birthday child's favorite farm animal. Make a sheep with coconut fleece and marshmallow legs or a chick with down of lemon-yellow frosting, a paper or candy corn beak, and candy eyes.

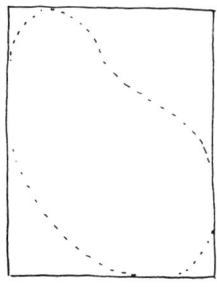 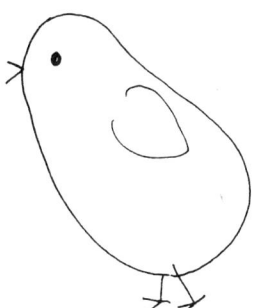

FAVORS
- Seed cups from *Planting Time*
- Plastic toy animals
- Cookie cutters in animal shapes
- Miniature tractors
- Coloring and activity books with farm themes
- Box of animal crackers
- Small pumpkins

Harvest Bowl

2 peeled, diced apples
Bunch of grapes
½ cup nuts
½ cup raisins
1 T. honey
½ t. cinnamon

Mix and serve in small bowls.

Scarecrow Shakes

2½ cups cold milk
2 ripe bananas
3 scoops (1½ cups) chocolate or vanilla ice cream
1 cup crushed ice (optional)

Mix in blender, blend at high speed 60 seconds, and serve at once. Makes 5 cups.

Mother Goose

*Hey diddle diddle, the cat and the fiddle
Are having a party today!*

INVITATIONS
- Choose a favorite nursery rhyme and reword it as an invitation. Example: "Wee Willie Winkie ran through the town/ Upstairs and downstairs in his nightgown./ Rapping at the window, crying through the lock/ Come to my birthday party!/ Be there at one o'clock."

- Write the party information on a page from a Mother Goose book or coloring book.
- Suggest that each guest bring something that a specific Mother Goose character would have.
  Examples:
  Wee Willie Winkie: slippers, nightgown, pajamas, or candle.

Little Miss Muffet: plastic spider or bowl and spoon.
Little Bo Peep: toy sheep, or a curved stick for a shepherd's crook.
Little Boy Blue: blue pants, jacket, or a toy horn.

DECORATIONS
- Play nursery rhyme records, available at the public library.
- Create Mother Goose scenes with appropriate props. Use one as a table centerpiece.
  Examples:
  Little Miss Muffet — a rubber spider hangs from the ceiling over a doll holding a bowl of cottage cheese.
  Humpty Dumpty — a hardboiled egg with a painted face and pipecleaner legs sits on a ledge or the mantel, with toy soldiers and horses below.
  Pussy In The Well — a cylinder of cardboard forms a well; make it big enough to hold a stuffed pussycat.
- Supply a box of old clothes for dress-up play.
- Set open books of Mother Goose rhymes around the party area.

ACTIVITIES
Mother Goose Parade
From a box of old clothes and trims, the guests add to their costumes. Then they form a parade, marching to music. Photos of this activity are good favors to send home.

Pin The Mouse On The Clock.
 The blindfolded players try to tape gray paper or felt mice at one o'clock on a large picture of a clock. Note: some young children do not like being blindfolded. Have them close their eyes, and ignore the peeking.

A Tisket, A Tasket
 Guests form a circle and sing:

A Tisket, A Tasket

A Tisket, A Tasket,
A green and yellow basket,
I wrote a letter to my love,
And on the way I lost it, I lost it,
And on the way I lost it.

 It walks around the outside of the circle, carrying a basket decorated with green and yellow ribbons and containing an envelope (the "letter to my love"). It places the basket behind one child, who then picks up the basket and runs after It. Both run around the circle, each trying to reach the empty spot. The one who does not reach the empty space becomes the next It.

Here We Go Round The Mulberry Bush
 Players join hands in a circle and walk around, singing "Mulberry Bush." They stop to demonstrate each activity as it is mentioned.

Mulberry Bush

Here we go round the mulberry bush, the mulberry bush, the mulberry bush. Here we go round the mulberry bush, so early in the morning.

This is the way we wash our face ...
Comb our hair ... Brush our teeth ... Put on our clothes ... Eat our food, etc.

Guess The Rhyme
Parent or helper acts out familiar rhymes, while the children guess them.

REFRESHMENTS
- Humpty Dumpty — Place a painted, egg-shaped cookie (see Crafts, page 147) on a slice of ice cream.

- Hot Cross Buns, Simple Simon pies, Little Jack Horner pies (each with a plum); Mother Goose is full of ideas — but steer clear of the curds and whey or peas porridge!
- Queen of Hearts Tarts (recipe follows).

Cake
- A frosted sheetcake with a Mother Goose scene. Use small toys, candies, marshmallows and raisins. Be sure each piece of cake includes one of the characters or part of the scene.

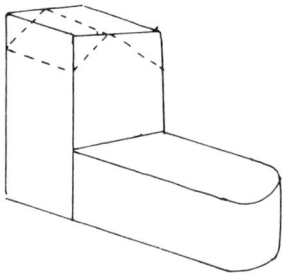 

- "The Old Woman Who Lived In A Shoe" cake. Cut a shoe shape and decorate it with licorice whip shoelaces, plastic babies, and a "granny doll" on top.

- "Peter, Peter, Pumpkin Eater's" home. Decorate a round cake with orange frosting and thin licorice strips. Use white frosting for window and door frames. This cake is especially appropriate for an October birthday.

FAVORS
- Use the "A Tisket, A Tasket" basket to hold favors for the birthday child to distribute as guests are leaving.
- Small Mother Goose rhyme books
- Small records with rhymes
- Miniature Mother Goose characters
- Photos of each child in costume
- Hard-boiled egg with Humpty Dumpty face

Queen of Hearts Tarts

1 package piecrust mix (or homemade piecrust)
Raspberry jam

Make piecrust dough and roll 1/8" thick on floured board. Cut in rounds or heart shapes. Place cut shapes on cookie sheet and put a spoonful of jam on each one. Cover each with another circle of dough. Seal edges and prick top crust with a fork. Bake at 450° for 10-12 minutes. When baked, sprinkle with red sugar or top with candy hearts.

Just a few of these ideas are plenty for a successful party.

Fire Engine #9

"...rolled out this morning lookin' mighty fine, goin' to a fire — you better be on time!"

INVITATIONS
- Cut a firefighter's hat from red construction paper and write "Tony's 4th Birthday" on the front. Put party details on the back.
- Make a firefighter's badge from sturdy paper; write the guest's name on the front and the party information on the back. Attach a safety pin to the badge so the guest can wear it to the party.

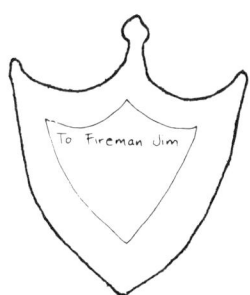

- Cut a card in the shape of a fire engine. Tape licorice pieces to form a hose ladder. Hand-deliver with care!

DECORATIONS
- Prop a ladder against an outside window and place large dolls on the rungs, climbing down the ladder or out the window. Place a stuffed animal wearing firefighter clothes (or hat) and holding a garden hose at the foot of the ladder.

- For a smaller indoor version of the above scene, use a toy house, popsicle-stick ladder, small dolls, and a toy fire engine.
- Make a fire engine by painting a refrigerator box, or other large box, with hooks, ladders, wheels, and hoses. Cut out one side of the box so the children can stand inside.
- Place toy fire engines and storybooks in the center of the party table and a fire hat at each place setting.
- Hang red, orange and yellow streamers and balloons throughout the room.

ACTIVITIES
Fire Truck Ride

While riding in the "firetruck" (see Decorations), the children take turns steering, carrying the stuffed fire engine dog, holding the ladder, and directing the hose at an imaginary fire. Play tape-recorded sirens and bells throughout.

Animal Toss

Guests pretend to be firefighters catching a stuffed dog jumping from a building. Wearing their fire hats, the children grasp the edge of a round tablecloth or piece of fabric and toss the toy upward, trampoline-style. The object is to see how many stuffed toys they can toss at one time, keeping them from falling to the floor.

Pin the Hat on the Firefighter

Another version of the ever-popular donkey's tail (see Games, page 134). Use sticky tape rather than pins or tacks to attach the red paper hats on the firefighter picture. The player whose hat comes closest to the target earns a round of applause.

Search & Rescue

Players search for hidden items such as plastic firefighter figures, red jelly beans, and candy corn. Each guest carries a container to hold the items found. Those who have found five items sit on the floor in a circle and wait for the others.

Arches

(See Games, page 129.)

Arrange for a tour of the neighborhood fire station. Guests may be allowed to climb aboard the actual fire truck. Some stations offer puppet shows as a public safety service. Some restaurants have party packages with food and favors geared to the firehouse theme.

REFRESHMENTS

- Mess kits (small shoeboxes) filled with goodies: peanut butter sandwiches, apple pieces, raisins, etc. Granola bars and nuts will give the young firefighters lots of extra energy.

Cake

- Fire engine or hat-shaped cake. Frost the cake in red. Trim with a licorice ladder and chocolate cookie wheels.

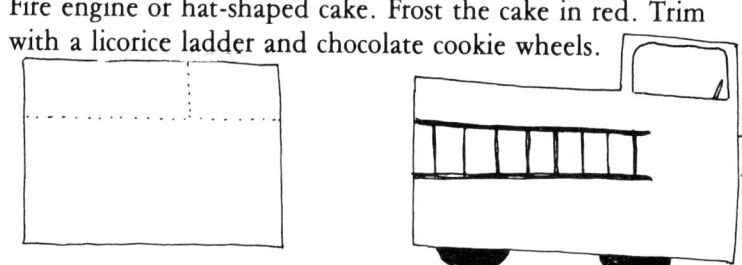

- Sheet cake decorated with a toy fire engine and small doll firefighters carrying licorice hoses. Use red tissue paper for flames, issuing from the windows of a toy house. For edible flames on a frosting house, use candy corn. Peanut butter cake is an all-time favorite (recipe follows).

FAVORS
- Toy firefighters, engines, etc.
- Red plastic firehats
- Long hoses of black licorice
- Firefighter's badge

Peanut Butter Cake

1 package yellow cake mix, non-pudding type
½ cup creamy peanut butter

Preheat oven to 350°. Prepare batter according to directions on package; add peanut butter. Pour batter into greased and floured 13" x 9" x 2" pan and bake 40 minutes or until a wooden pick inserted comes out clean. Cool and spread with creamcheese frosting.

Creamcheese frosting

1-oz. package creamcheese, softened
¼ cup creamy peanut butter
2 t. vanilla
½ t. salt
2-2½ cups sifted powdered sugar

Beat creamcheese, vanilla, peanut butter, and salt until fluffy. Gradually beat in sugar until the mixture is of spreading consistency. Guaranteed to please all peanut butter fans!

Alphabet Fun

*"Now I've said my ABCs;
tell me what you think of me."*

INVITATIONS
- Cut a card in the shape of the birthday child's initial, and print: "The letter A is happy to announce Ann's birthday."
- Ask each guest to bring a simple item that starts with a favorite letter. If the letter chosen by the guest is A, for example, the item might be an apple, ant, anklet, or angleworm.

DECORATIONS
- Tape or staple large, colorful paper letters to dowels. Stick them in the ground to form an alphabet garden leading to the party entrance.

- Draw or paint a large letter on a heavy cardboard box. Cut openings with a utility knife, forming an entryway for guests to crawl through. This also forms a playhouse for the birthday child to keep.

- Stack alphabet blocks for the table centerpiece.
- Make cardboard letters or purchase a folding alphabet set from an educational outlet. Tape the letters on the walls or hang them from the ceiling on long strings.
- Attach magnetic letters to a board or to metal objects in the party area.
- Place alphabet books within easy reach of guests.

ACTIVITIES

Cookie Letter Bake

Using a simple, pre-mixed dough (recipe follows), guests form their own cookies in the shapes of letters. Use cookie cutters or make cardboard letter patterns. Help each guest to cut three or four letters and place them in the oven to bake during other activities. The children will enjoy singing the Alphabet Song while they make their cookies. If more than four children are present, get a helper to assist with this activity.

Guess The Letter

Guests take turns showing the items brought and guessing the letters they begin with.

Make A Letter

In this alternative to *Cookie Letter Bake,* guests are given chunks of Baker's Clay (see Crafts, page 148) and, on a paper-covered table or floor, form the letters of their own names or other favorite letters. Reserve some of the clay for the party's last activity.

Alphabet Puppet Show

The parent or helper uses hand puppets to tell a story (see *Perfect Purple Parrot*, Games, page 143).

Who Has The Letters?

(See *Dog & Bone*, Games, page 130.) One child sits in the box used as an entryway, while another child quietly takes the alphabet block placed beside the box.

Cookie Letter Hunt

Guests hunt for hidden letter-shaped cookies. Assist the shyer children, so everyone finds at least one cookie to eat or keep.

People Alphabet

In groups of two or three, players use their bodies to form letters on the floor. Adult guidance may be needed.

More Letters

The children return to the Baker's Clay, where they make whatever they like until it's time to go home.

REFRESHMENTS

- Sandwiches ("P"-nut butter, what else?), cut in the shapes of various letters with cookie cutters.
- Alphabet edibles: alphabet soup, alphabet cereal, etc.

Cake

- Letter cake. Cut a sheet cake into a large letter, forming the birthday child's initial, and frost it with a favorite flavor.
- Cupcakes frosted with various letters or with each guest's initial. Letter-shaped candles are available in some variety stores.

FAVORS
- Cookies from *Cookie Letter Bake*.
- Baker's Clay letters.
- Small items with guests' names or initials: necklaces, pins, barrettes, wooden letters, etc.
- ABC books and alphabet coloring books.

. . . .

Ashley's Alphabet Cookies

A good dough for cutting shapes

1 cup sugar
1 cup light molasses
1 cup shortening
1 T. vinegar
6 cups sifted flour
½ t. salt
½ t. baking powder
1 t. each baking soda, ginger, and cinnamon
2 beaten eggs

    Combine sugar, molasses, shortening and vinegar in saucepan; bring to a boil, cook 2 minutes, and set aside to cool. Sift together flour, baking powder, baking soda, and spices. Add eggs to cooled molasses mixture. Add flour mixture and stir well. Wrap and chill the dough. Roll ¼ inch thick on lightly floured board. Cut into shapes. Place on lightly greased baking sheet and bake at 375° 8-10 minutes. When cool, decorate with frosting, candy sprinkles, raisins, or chocolate chips.

Sesame Street

INVITATIONS
- Make a card from brightly-colored paper and write, "Come along with me to Maria's house for an hour of birthday fun with all your friends from Sesame Street."
- Buy Big Bird, Grover, or Cookie Monster invitations and cut them into four or five pieces to form a puzzle.
- Drop a finger puppet with an invitation inside into each guest's mailbox.
- Send a page from a Sesame Street coloring book. Have the guests color the page and bring it to the party to add to the decorations. Stretch a string across one wall of the party room and clip the pictures to it.

DECORATIONS
- Display the birthday child's Sesame Street dolls, puppets, books, etc. as centerpieces and decorations.
- Play Sesame Street records.
- Create Big Bird's nest in one corner of the party area, using yellow blankets or pillows. The guests can take turns sitting in it, and the birthday child can open presents while "nesting" in it.

- Make a Sesame Street scene with large boxes labeled "Mr. Hooper's Store," "Oscar's Garbage Can," "Mr. Snuffle-upagus' Cave," "Maria's apartment," etc. For a miniature Sesame Street scene, use shoeboxes and dolls.
- Use commercial decorations, available in variety and card shops.

ACTIVITIES

Grover's Groovy Shapes
   While waiting for all the guests to arrive, the children point out various geometric shapes. These are triangles, circles, and squares cut from colored paper and taped to lamps, light switches, and furniture.

Sherlock Hemlock
   Guests search for Sesame Street puppets, dolls and stuffed animals that have been hidden behind chairs, curtains, etc. As soon as a toy is found, it is brought to "Big Bird's nest" (see Decorations) and the child who found it sits on the floor as part of a circle for the next activity. This game can also be used as a search for favors the children may take home.

Snuffle-upagus Ring Pass
   (see Ring On The String, page 130.)

Kermit's Big Time Theater
   Guests are entertained by the birthday child's older brothers and sisters, who present a puppet show with Sesame Street characters.

Oscar Over The Garbage Can
   (See *Charlie Over The Water,* Games, page 130.)
   Use the following words:
>   "Oscar over the Garbage Can,
>   Oscar Over the Sea,
>   Oscar caught a mousy
>   But he can't catch me!"

Pudding Pictures
   (See Crafts, page 147.)

Bert and Ernie Exercises
   The children follow the parent in simple exercises — reaching high, touching toes, stretching from side to side, making airplane propellers with arms going round and round. Use this if you feel the guests need to get the wiggles out.

What's Missing?
   One of the guests (a volunteer) goes out of the room with the parent or helper and removes a sock, shoe, hair ribbon, or party hat. When the volunteer returns, the others must guess what is missing. The one who guesses correctly becomes the next to leave the room and remove an item.

REFRESHMENTS
- Ginger Cookies (see Ashley's Alphabet Cookies, page 20). Decorate with frosting and candy sprinkles.
- Party Punch (recipe follows).

Cake
- Sesame Street character cake, baked in specially-shaped, purchased pan. Frost and decorate with coconut, candies, and Sesame Street figures.

FAVORS
- Sesame Street finger puppets
- Pictures created in the *Pudding Pictures* activity.
- Sesame Street books, records, figures, and coloring and activity books.

. . . .

Party Punch

½ cup cranberry juice drink
½ cup orange juice
1 scoop vanilla ice cream

Mix juices in cup. Add ice cream. Serve with a straw. Makes one serving.

Land of Make Believe

Once long ago, in a land far away, there lived elves, fairies, gnomes, pixies, and leprechauns ... with this party, you can join them for an enchanting afternoon or evening in Fairyland.

INVITATIONS
- Inside or on the front of a folded card, tape a magic wand made from a toothpick topped with a gummed silver star. Under the wand, write: "Shhh, listen — the fairies and elves are having a special birthday party for Angela, and you are invited!"
- Under a rainbow colored by the birthday child on a square of white paper, write: "Fly over the rainbow to a birthday party in the Land of Make Believe."
- If the party's theme is a particular fairy tale, send a picture or item from that story.
  Examples —
   Cinderella: glass slipper
   Jack and the Beanstalk: card with a cow on the front and a handful of real beans inside.
- A shamrock or a box of Irish green soap with a green card are ideas for a leprechaun's invitation (especially near St. Patrick's Day).

DECORATIONS

- Cut a large cardboard arrow. With black felt pen, write "To Fairyland" or "To The Land of Make Believe" on it. Attach the arrow to a stick or dowel, hang wispy streamers around it, and stand it at the party entrance.
- Scatter confetti in a path of "fairy footprints" for guests to follow to the party area.
- Make a tunnel by opening both ends of a large cardboard box; this is the entrance to Fairyland. Hang beads or strips of colored paper over the opening. As the guests crawl through the tunnel, they are sprinkled with imaginary fairy dust or touched on the head with a magic wand (plastic straw wrapped in aluminum foil) by the birthday child.

- Hang paper clouds, moon, and aluminum foil stars (made by the birthday child) on strings from the ceiling. Drape them with angel hair, out of reach of inquisitive fingers.
- If this is an evening party, hang Christmas twinkle lights in the trees or shrubs.
- Plant a garden of giant flowers and toadstools against trees, shrubs or a back fence. They're easy to make, using tagboard or construction paper for petals and leaves, and green garden stakes for stems.

- On a large sheet of cardboard or tagboard, spray or brush paint a colorful rainbow, and cut out the arc under it. This makes an archway for guests to walk or crawl under.
- Make a gumdrop tree by hanging small bags of gumdrops on tree branches, using Christmas tree ornament hooks. We once made a gumdrop tree by throwing the candy directly onto a pine tree. Believe it or not, it worked beautifully.
- Make a sunken well by placing a bowl of lemonade or Fairy Nectar (recipe follows) in dry ice surrounded by ivy or other greens. Guests can sip the fairy nectar through multi-colored straws that have been labeled with their names. Use care when handling dry ice.

ACTIVITIES

Fairy Crowns and Elf Caps

Guests color and decorate their own fairy crowns or elf caps (see *Hats,* Crafts, page 150).

Give the Fairy a Wand

This version of *Pin the Tail on the Donkey* (see Games, page 134) requires a large poster or drawing that pictures a fairy-like creature and wands made of cardboard. A bit of glue and glitter on each wand adds a magic sparkle. Use sticky tape on the wands instead of pins or tacks.

Alternatives:

"Pin the Horn on the Unicorn"

"Pin the Shamrock on the Leprechaun"

"Pin the Shoes on the Pixie"

Enchanted Webs

Players search for small pixie figurines (or edible treats in plastic bags), one for each guest, throughout the yard or room. Each pixie or bag has a different-colored long piece of yarn or string attached; the other end of the yarn is tied to a square of stiff cardboard with a guest's name on it. Trail the yarns, spider-web fashion, around the area, intermingling the colors — a decorative sight. The guests wind the yarn around their pieces of cardboard until they finally reach the prizes. Those who finish first help the others.

Pot o' Gold

Players take turns "fishing" in a pot of gold, using a fishnet or a stick with string and cup hook attached. The pot is a large flowerpot or other bowl spray-painted gold or covered with gold foil and placed at the end of a rainbow made from crepe paper, cardboard, or plywood. The pot is filled with small bags of gold-covered chocolate coins or other "fishable" treats. A helper can make sure each hook picks up a bag, so everyone is a winner.

Brownies and Fairies
(see Games, page 133.)

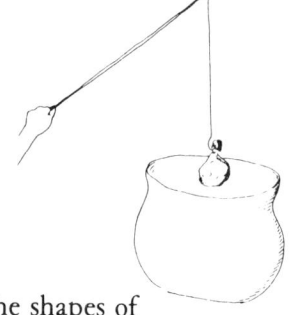

REFRESHMENTS
- Sandwiches cut with cookie cutters into the shapes of butterflies, flowers, toadstools, hearts or stars.
- Pink lemonade or Fairy Nectar (recipe follows)
- Vegetables or fruits cut in miniature slices and served on doll plates or nasturtium leaves (yes, they are edible).

Cake
- Fairy cake, made by placing a doll in the center of a baked angelfood cake. Frost the cake to resemble a full, white skirt, and tape white felt wings to the doll. Place a cardboard-and-glitter crown on her head and a toothpick wand with a gummed star on the tip in her hand.

- Graham cracker house (see "Making Miniatures," page 70).
- Castle cake (see "Knights & Dragons," page 105).
- Rainbow cake. Frost a sheet cake in white. Decorate it with a frosting rainbow. Use yellow frosting or gold foil for a pot of gold, and beside it stand a doll fairy with a wand.

- Cupcakes with Thumbelina on each one — a tiny plastic baby doll in a nutshell.

FAVORS
- Items useful to fairies and elves, such as sacks of fairy dust (gold glitter) and magic wands
- Crowns and caps made by the guests
- Pixies or other prizes found in "Enchanted Webs"
- Fairy kits, packed in small painted or aluminum foil-covered boxes. Include wings, wand, crown, fairy dust, etc.

. . . .

Fairy Nectar

1 6-oz. can frozen lemonade, thawed
1 46-oz. can fruit juice drink
1 quart lemon-lime carbonated beverage, chilled
1 quart raspberry sherbet

Mix liquids; spoon sherbet into bowl when ready to serve. Makes 14 servings.

Just a few of these ideas are plenty for a successful party.

All Aboard

INVITATIONS
- Make an engineer's hat (see Crafts, page 157). Write the party information on the back and leave the front to be colored by the guest. The hat can be worn to the party.

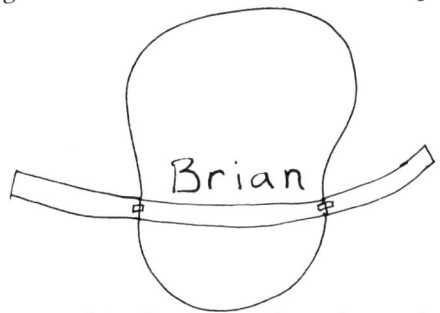

- Form a card in the shape of a suitcase, lantern, railroad crossing sign, or old-fashioned locomotive.
- Send a ticket good for a "ride on the birthday express" to be brought to the party. Have extras!

DECORATIONS
- With black chalk, draw a train track on the front walk.
- If invitations are tickets, form a booth from an appliance box, where the guests turn their tickets in as admission to the party.
- Set up a toy train in a corner of the party area.
- Pile suitcases with travel stickers in one corner.
- Tape travel posters and train pictures to the walls.

ACTIVITIES

Train Time

Early arrivals can be happily occupied watching or playing with toy train sets. If it's electric, be sure the train set is working. One grandmother we know found dismay and frustration when faced with a lame train!

All Aboard

When all the guests have arrived, they form a line. Calling "All aboard," and with the birthday child as the engineer, the children "choo choo" in a circle around the room to music until the announcement is made that "the train is arriving at Tom's party in one minute." The train stops and everyone gets off the track, ready for the next activity.

Make a Train

Each guest is given four or five pieces of construction paper, pre-cut into boxcar, engine, and caboose shapes. On another, larger sheet of paper, they assemble and paste their trains, using Lifesavers for wheels, cotton for smoke, licorice for a cowcatcher, and a gumdrop for a headlight.

Stop the Train

In this variation of *Musical Chairs* (see Games, page 134), two rows of chairs are lined side by side, facing one direction. To train music, the players march around the chairs, scrambling for a seat when the music stops.

Railroad Ride

Players climb into four or five open cardboard boxes, lined up train fashion, and pretend they are going for a train ride. Each takes a turn at being the engineer or conductor.

For a party away from home, several sites offer train themes. Amtrak stations, certain restaurants, amusement parks, and zoos are possibilities.

REFRESHMENTS
- Box lunches with peanut butter and jam sandwiches and fruit.
- Fruit juice or milk
- Tangerine Yogurt Dip (recipe follows)

Cake
- Ice cream cake with train motif, available at ice cream specialty shops such as Baskin-Robbins.
- Locomotive cake. Use a loaf-shaped cake for the main section and round ice cream sandwiches (available at Baskin-Robbins and other ice cream outlets) for the front. Strips of licorice or chocolate cookies make wheels, and a large yellow gumdrop is the headlight. Add other trims made from paper or small candies.

- Boxcars. Cut a sheet cake into separate railroad cars, each labeled with the name of a guest and topped with candy favors. Use cookies for wheels. (See "Hobo Heaven" cake, page 110).
- Train track cake. Frost a sheet cake with plain white icing and lay a track of licorice rope across it. Place a toy train on the tracks and let your creativity take over in designing a scene around it. Gumdrop and toothpick trees, green coconut grass, toy barns and animals, and animal crackers are examples.

FAVORS
- Miniature suitcases or travel bags
- Train books or records
- Toy boxcars (see Crafts, page 199) filled with candies, nuts or raisins

Tangerine Yogurt Dip

3 tangerines
6 lettuce leaves
3 cups fruit-flavored yogurt

Peel tangerines, and break them into sections. Make a circle of tangerine sections on the lettuce. Spoon yogurt into the center of the circle. Sections are dipped in yogurt and eaten. Serves 6.
Bananas, apples, or grapes may be substituted for tangerines.

A Teddy Bears' Picnic

INVITATIONS
- Cut paper dolls (see Crafts, page 47) in bear shapes, and put a portion of the invitation on each of the connected bears.
- Cut a card into a basket shape, with a slot that holds a removable bear. Write the invitation on the bear.

- Form a card into the shape of a bear holding a basket. Write party details inside.
- Hand-deliver a paper basket (see Crafts, page 149) with a party invitation and a few candy "Gummy Bears" in it.
- Invite guests to dress up their own teddy bears and bring them to the picnic.

DECORATIONS
- Collect every bear you can find, in any size, shape or condition. Hide them among trees, bushes and furniture in the

party area, and place one by the door as "greeter." The very old, venerable bears can have a reserved place of honor, just for them.
- Place a large blanket or picnic cloth on the lawn or other party area. Put each guest's lunch individually packed in a small basket or paper bag labeled with the guest's name.

ACTIVITIES

Say Hello to Teddy

Guests seat their bears on the picnic cloth and introduce them to the others.

Count the Bears

Guests find the hidden teddy bears — counting, not collecting them.

Teddy Bear Contest

Each child's teddy bear sits on the picnic cloth and receives a prize as the oldest, smallest, largest, most unusual, fattest, best-dressed, etc. Be sure each teddy gets an award — gummed stars or bear stickers.

Find the Cinnamon Bear

Guests search for the ginger cookie bears (see Ashley's Alphabet Cookies, page 20) hidden throughout the party area. Have extras on hand for those who find only a few. The cookies go into the individual picnic baskets or bags.

Pin the Bow on Teddy

Guests take turns being blindfolded (or just closing their eyes), spun three times, and sent in the direction of a jolly teddy bear drawn on a large sheet of paper. Everyone has a red paper bow with double-sided sticky tape and tries to attach it to the bear's collar. Applause is awarded the one who comes closest to the center of the collar.

Hidden Bears

Guests sit in a circle with the bears in the middle. One child leaves the room. Another child hides a teddy bear. The first child returns and is allowed three chances to guess which bear is missing and three chances to guess who it belongs to. Be sure each player gets to be It or hide a teddy bear.

REFRESHMENTS

- Picnic fare, in baskets or bags: peanut butter sandwiches, raisins, nuts, carrot sticks, and small cans of juice.

Cake

- Picnic Cake. Decorate a sheet cake with marshmallow-and-toothpick bears, gumdrop trees, green coconut grass, and tiny baskets set on a multi-colored "cloth" of flat candies. Stand ginger cookie bears around the sides.
- Teddy Bear Cake. Bake a standard cake, chocolate or spice, in a 13" x 9" pan. Cut as shown. Put the pieces together with chocolate frosting (save enough for the top). Frost the bear's nose, paws, and tummy in white and sprinkle liberally with coconut. Frost the rest of the bear with chocolate. Use round candies for the eyes and nose and thin licorice strips for the mouth.

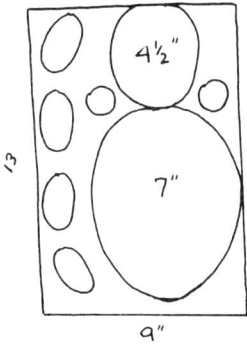 

FAVORS

- Picnic baskets or bags, labeled with guests' names
- Ginger cookie bears
- Bear stickers
- "Gummy Bears" — small candy bears
- Since the teddies, too, are party guests, they deserve favors of their own, such as tightly sealed, miniature jars of honey, tucked into the lunch baskets.

Tiaras and Top Hats

Time to play dress-up!

INVITATIONS
- On a single sheet of plain white, heavy paper, use black or gold ink for the formal wording. Write with flourishes or in calligraphy. For example:
    Miss Jennifer Ann Jones requests the Honor of your Presence at the Celebration of her Sixth Birthday on the First of June, Nineteen Hundred and Eighty-Four. 1234 S.E. Fairview Street, Portland, Oregon. RSVP 272-6834. Please wear formal attire ("dressup" costume).
- Cut pictures of formally dressed people from magazines (a good job for the birthday child) and paste them on the front of a handmade, folded card, with party details inside.
- On the front of the invitation, copy or paste a picture of a child playing dress-up.
- Draw a top hat or other item suggesting a formal occasion, form a card from it, and write the party information inside.

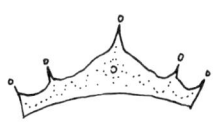 

DECORATIONS
- Real or artificial flowers in formal bouquets
- Tall candles
- Tablecloth (or white sheet) and napkins
- Spotlight, to play on guests as they arrive
- Formally dressed, large dolls seated in a corner of the room or at the birthday table

ACTIVITIES
Limo Service

Parent or helper chauffeurs the guests to the party.

Announcing Arrivals

A helper dressed in a suit, tux, or tails formally announces the guests' names as they arrive (Kathryn Louise Moore of Baker Street; Ryan Marshall Thompson of 68th Avenue, etc.)

Dress Up

Pull out the trunk or box of dress-up items for guests to adorn themselves. It should include costume jewelry, gloves, scarves, high heels, bow ties, hats, and long skirts. A feather boa is a nice touch.

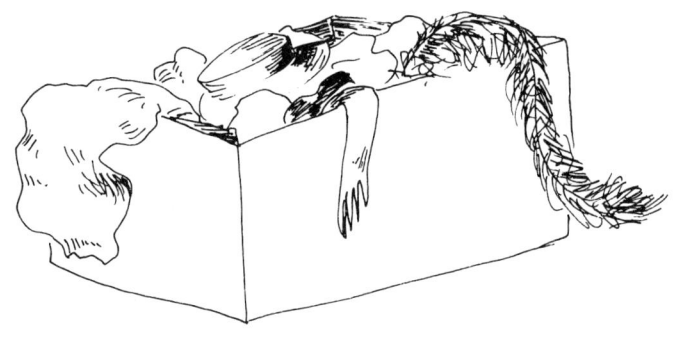

Hat Shop

Purchase felt hats at a thrift store or novelty store, or make hats from fabric (see Crafts, page 160). Give a hat to each guest and provide plenty of glue, feathers, ribbons, scraps of material, bells, artificial flowers, sequins, etc., for decorating the hats.

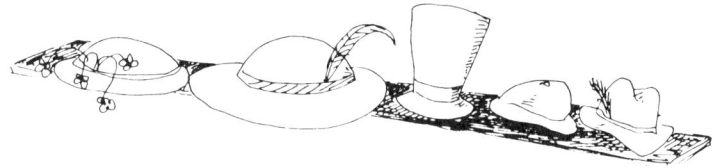

Fashion Show

After they're costumed, guests form a line and parade through the party area. Have a mirror handy, and don't forget the camera!

Bag of Clothes

(See Games, page 136.)

REFRESHMENTS

- Tea sandwiches: cut bread rounds with a biscuit or cookie cutter. Fill the small sandwiches with cream cheese or butter and cucumber slices, cheese, thin ham slices, peanut butter, egg salad, or jelly.
- Tea with lemon slices, sugar cubes, honey or lemon drops
- Fancy Tea Cookies (recipe follows)
- Colored mints on a tray
- Mixed fancy nuts

Cake

- Sheet cake, frosted in white and decorated with silver leaves and pink frosting roses.
- Top hat. Make four round cakes. Frost each with chocolate frosting and stack them. Use black paper to make the brim of the hat.
- Ice cream cake topped with fancy flowers, available at Baskin-Robbins.

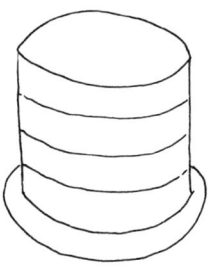 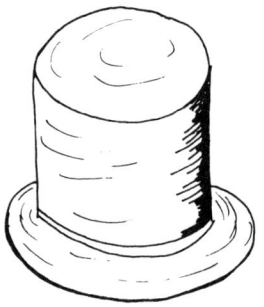

FAVORS

- Hats the guests have trimmed
- Photos of guests in their costumes and hats
- Top hats and canes, available in variety stores
- Tiaras, purchased in toy or costume shops, or handmade (see Crafts, page 132)
- Play makeup kits
- Old costume jewelry
- Artificial or real corsages and boutonnieres

. . . .

Fancy Tea Cookies

1 cup butter or margarine
½ cup powdered sugar
2 cups flour
1 t. vanilla
¼ t. salt
1 cup chopped walnuts

Cream butter and sugar until fluffy. Gradually mix in flour. Stir in vanilla, salt and nuts. Shape mixture into balls, using one level tablespoon. Place on ungreased cookie sheet and bake at 400° for 10-12 minutes, until done but not browned. When cool, roll in powdered sugar. (About 4 dozen cookies)

Home on the Range

"where seldom is heard a discouraging word..."

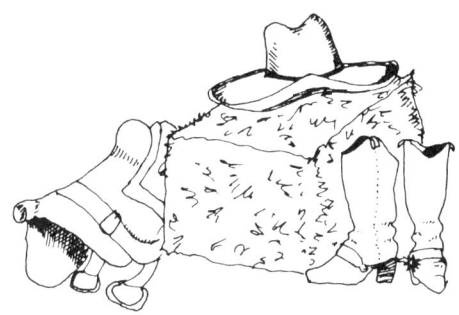

INVITATIONS
- Cut construction paper cards in shapes related to a cowboy theme: a stetson hat, gun, boot with spur, horse, Indian headdress, sheriff's badge, bandit or Lone Ranger mask are a few ideas.

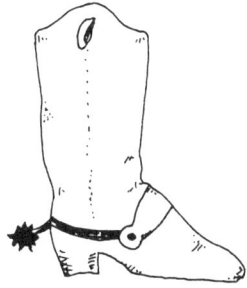

- Write the invitation as a rodeo ticket. Request that the ticket be brought to the party for a door-prize drawing. (Have extra tickets available for those who forget.)
- On the invitations, tell guests to come to the party in wild west attire. Have extra hats, scarves, and Indian headbands on hand.

DECORATIONS
- Prop tagboard tombstones in the area leading to the party entrance — especially effective on a front lawn. Label the tombstones with famous names from the wild west: Calamity Jane, Buffalo Bill, Annie Oakley, etc.
- Create a wild west scene by making a fence, cactus, etc., from tagboard or cardboard.

- Cover chairs with Indian blankets, if available.
- Paint an old sheet with Indian designs (fun for the birthday child), using crayons, acrylics, or felt pens. Draped over a card table, the sheet becomes a tepee.
- Put an Indian tepee by each place at the table. To make a tepee, turn a pointed paper cup or sugar cone upside down. Cut the point off and glue toothpicks in the top as tent poles. Write each child's name on the outside of the tepee, and place a small favor under each cup.

- Make a western wagon by tying a bale of hay in a child's wagon.
- Form a "town jail" from a refrigerator box. With a utility knife, cut a barred window and entrance and exit doors. Place the jail in or near the entrance to the party area.

- Place a saddle on a sawhorse; add a hobby horse head and a yarn tail.
- Dress dolls and stuffed animals in red bandanas, cowboy hats, headbands, or sunbonnets. Seat some of them in the haywagon as a pioneer family. Others might form a band of Indians hiding behind the cacti.
- Decorate the table with log cabins made of toy logs and covered wagons from baskets with handles. The cover of the

wagon is stiff paper tucked under the basket's handle. Glue black felt or paper circles for wheels. Place party treats in the baskets, which can be taken home by the guests.

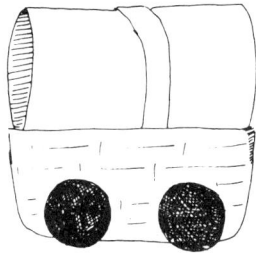

- If adults are included in the party, invite them to wear western costumes, too.

ACTIVITIES
With several activities going on at one time, guests can join the ones they prefer.

Into the Hoosegow

Everyone entering the party must first be jailed, with freedom just one word away. The name of the Lone Ranger's horse (Silver) is the password. Give one clue: "Hi-yo ..."

Westward Ho

Riding in the pioneers' haywagon, pulled by the Wagonmaster, is a thrill. As the wagon makes its way through the garage, backyard, or basement, the Wagonmaster warns of impending dangers: "Westward Ho, on to Oregon! Keep a lookout for hazards.... There's a buffalo stampede ... and a band of Indians on the warpath. Everybody duck ... we made it. Everyone out of the wagon — we have to swim across this deep river. Finally, we're on the other side ... now for the final stretch, up these mountains. Over the top ... and down. We made it!"

Sutter's Mill
>With pie tins, guests take turns panning for gold (spray-painted rocks or gold sequins) in a plastic wading pool partially filled with water.

Giddyap
>Children take turns riding the horse (sawhorse or bale of hay with a blanket or saddle thrown over it), held by a parent or helper. Add a little excitement with a few bounces, "giddyaps," and "whoas."

Indian Headdress
>(See *Hats,* Crafts, page 50)

Horse Race
>(see *Wheelbarrow Relay,* Games, page 40.)

Roundup
>A variation of Tag; each tagged child is put into a corral.

Around the Campfire
>After refreshments are served and eaten, guests gather around the "campfire" (barbecue or imitation fire; see "Hobo Heaven," page 68), and listen to cowboy stories read or told by an adult. They smoke the peace pipe (bubble pipes) and sing songs, including *Home on the Range.*

Visit a western-style restaurant for refreshments.

REFRESHMENTS
- If the weather allows, cook over an open fire or barbecue in the yard. Serve foods in tin cans or on pie tins.
- Hamburgers, hot dogs, sloppy joes, beef jerky, stew, or mild chili with crackers are good choices for cowboy appetites.

- Fresh fruit
- Plain or chocolate milk served in coffee mugs or camping cups

Cake
- For a "prairie schooner" cake, check with specialty ice cream shops such as Baskin-Robbins. Order an ice cream roll cake covered with white frosting and frosted in chocolate on the ends. Add chocolate cookies for wheels.
- Cowboy hat cake. Cut a sheet cake in the shape of a cowboy hat, frost it with lemon yellow icing, and pipe chocolate as trim.
- Corral cake (recipe follows). Around the edges of the frosted sheet cake build a fence of licorice pieces, sticks of chewing gum, or toothpicks and yarn. Place miniature horses, cows, sheep, etc., in the corral.

FAVORS
- Indian headdresses, made by guests
- Cowboy hats
- Miniature covered wagons filled with candies, nuts, or popcorn
- Peace pipe (bubble pipes)
- Gold nuggets, panned in *Sutter's Mill* game
- Lone Ranger masks/badges
- Sheriff's badges
- Photos of guests in jail or in the hay wagon
- Miniature cowboy or horse figures

Corral Cake

½ cup butter or margarine
¾ cup honey
⅔ cup brown sugar
2 eggs
2 cups whole wheat flour
½ cup soy flour
1 t. each cinnamon, baking soda, salt
½ t. each nutmeg and allspice
⅔ cup yogurt or buttermilk
2 t. vanilla
¾ cup chopped nuts
1 cup ripe mashed bananas or 4 peeled, chopped apples

Cream butter, honey and sugar. Add eggs; beat until fluffy. Mix dry ingredients together and add alternately with vanilla and yogurt to butter mixture. Stir in fruit and nuts. Bake in 13″ x 9″ greased pan at 350 degrees for 30 minutes. Test for doneness with toothpick.

Frosting

2 T. butter   2-3 T. milk or buttermilk
¼ cup honey   1 cup instant powdered milk
1 t. vanilla   ¼ t. each cinnamon, nutmeg, and allspice

Beat until smooth. For fruit frosting, substitute fruit juice for milk and add grated orange or lemon rind.

Wizard of Oz

"We're off to see the Wizard ...
The wonderful Wizard of Oz!"

INVITATIONS

- Draw a rainbow on a folded card of white or light blue construction paper. The birthday child colors the rainbow or leaves it blank for the guests to color and bring to the party to add to the decorations.
- Cut red construction paper in the shape of a ruby slipper. Glue sequins or glitter on it and write "Follow the Yellow Brick Road to a birthday party in the Emerald City."
- On a plain white folded card, draw a yellow brick road leading to a rainbow. Party information goes inside the card.

Note: If you plan to use permanent marking pens in the *Favorites of Oz* activity, inform the guests (or their parents) so the children can dress accordingly.

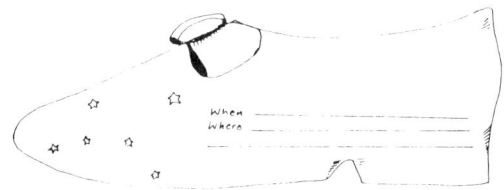

DECORATIONS

- Use a long piece of yellow butcher paper to represent the Yellow Brick Road; outline bricks with black felt pen. Tape the paper to the walk leading to the party entrance.
- Hang a large cardboard sign that reads "Welcome, Visitors, to the Land of Oz"

- Crepe paper streamers, balloons, napkins, and centerpiece should be Emerald City green ... or in all colors of the rainbow.
- Cover a large armchair with green fabric or crepe paper. This is the Wizard's throne, where the guests take turns sitting and the birthday child sits to open presents.
- In one corner of the room, place a large doll dressed in frilly material, with a star-tipped wand in her hand. This is Glinda, the Good Witch of the East.
- In another corner pile the remains of the Wicked Witch of the West; a small bucket of water, a black pointed hat, shoes, and a broom were all that was left when the witch melted.
- Set a toy castle on the floor or a table to represent either the palace in the Emerald City or the witch's castle.

ACTIVITIES

Going to Oz

As the guests approach the entrance to the party area, they are told to close their eyes and imagine they are Dorothy, about to be caught up in a tornado and deposited in the Land of Oz. An electric fan, hidden nearby, is switched on and the guests are "blown" into the party. A recording of tornado sounds may be available at the public library.

Favorites of Oz

Place a plain white sheet on a table or the floor. Provide guests with permanent or watercolor pens for drawing their favorite scenes from *The Wizard of Oz*. This can be the tablecloth when refreshments are served, as well as a souvenir of the party for the birthday child.

Follow the Yellow Brick Road

In this version of Follow the Leader, guests take turns being Dorothy, who carries a stuffed dog to represent Toto.

Dorothy leads the group around the room, past the castle and witches, etc., ending at the spot where the next activity will take place.

Scarecrow and Tinman Snicklefritz
(See *Snicklefritz,* Games, page 131.)

Cowardly Lion Marshmallow Race
Use a section of the Yellow Brick Road for a marshmallow race (see *Ping Pong Blow,* Games, page 141).

Story Time
Rent a videotape or film (90 minutes) of *The Wizard of Oz,* or read aloud a shortened version of the story.

Meet The Wizard

This should be the party's last activity, after refreshments and gifts. A parent or helper hides behind curtains or in a closet near the throne. Guests gather around the throne and hear the booming voice say, "Guests of Holly's birthday party, you have approached the throne of the Great and Wonderful Wizard of Oz. Before you can leave, you must tell me the three gifts I gave to Dorothy's friends." (The children answer that the lion received courage, the tin woodman was given a heart, and the scarecrow received brains.)

The Wizard's voice is heard again: "Very good. Now you will receive your gifts from Oz." (The birthday child then distributes the gifts as they are mentioned.) "Jelly beans, to be taken as needed for courage ... a heart for a heart ... and a diploma for brains. Now — close your eyes, click your heels together three times, and say, 'there's no place like home.'"

Treats in hand, the guests do as bidden. And the party is over.

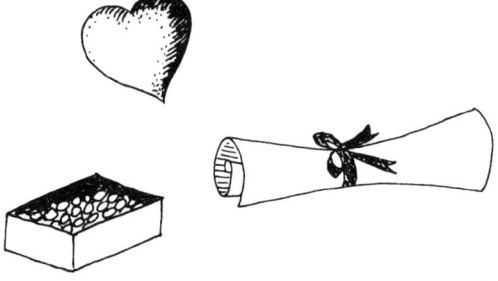

Courage: small green jelly beans in boxes or plastic bags.
Heart: any heart-shaped item (candy, stickers, soap, etc.).
Brains: rolled-up paper tied with a green ribbon.

REFRESHMENTS
- Anything you can color green. Add food coloring to cottage cheese, yogurt, ice cream, milk.
- Lime jello, celery with peanut butter, green grapes, minted pears, chocolate-mint ice cream
- Rainbow sherbet
- Rainbow Punch (recipe follows)
- Limeade, lemonade

Cake
- Cupcakes topped with multi-colored candies, representing a rainbow
- Sheet cake with a yellow brick road of cookies or butter mints. Color and cut out a paper rainbow and stand it over the road. Place a tiny pair of doll slippers at one end of the rainbow.

FAVORS
- Treats from *Meet The Wizard* activity
- Rainbow stickers
- *Wizard of Oz* coloring and activity books

Rainbow Punch

Fill three ice cube trays with various colors of juice: lime, cranberry, orange, or grape.

Put one cube of each color into glass and fill with orangeade, or apple juice.

Just a few of these ideas are plenty for a successful party.

Under the Big Top

Come to the second-greatest show on earth!

INVITATIONS
- On a card, make a lion's head with its mouth wide open. Between the jaws, write: "Welcome back from the Circus Safari! Your search for the rarest and most ferocious animals of the world is over. Now you're invited to Matthew's Birthday Circus Extravaganza. Bring your circus animal that will fit in our shoebox cages."

- Blow up a balloon and write the invitation on it with soft felt pen. Then deflate the balloon and send it with a note to blow up the balloon.

- Make a cage by partially cutting one side of an envelope to form ¼" wide bars; color the bars black (or see *Lanterns*, page 153). Put a tiger picture on a card that fits inside a cage. Write the party information on the back of the tiger. Place the tiger in the cage and mail both in an envelope.

- Draw a circus tent on a folded paper card and cut an opening as the big top's entrance. Leave one side of the entrance uncut so it will fold shut. Fit four tickets into the opening, as admission to party events: Umbrella Toss, Hungry Clown, etc. (see *Carnival* activity).

DECORATIONS
- If guests have been asked to bring their safari animals, make one cage for each animal. Cage-making is a good pre-party activity for the birthday child. Staple or tape black strips of paper across the top of an opened shoe box. Make the strips long enough to fold under the bottom of the box.
- Place three plates turned upside-down on the table, to represent a 3-ring circus. Arrange a different performing act on each plate. Examples: use modeling clay to help balance a plastic dog on a golf ball; put a drinking straw in a piece of clay and place a small toy monkey atop the straw, doing a handstand. Have enough plastic circus animals and performers so the guests can each take one home as a favor.

- Attach a balloon to each child's chair. Write the guest's name on the balloon. Have extras.
- Drape streamers across the ceiling.
- Ask helpers to be the Tattooed Lady (draw tattoos with watercolor pencils and removable decals), the Strong Man carrying weights, and a clown juggling two or three oranges.

ACTIVITIES
Circus Animals
As guests arrive, they place the animals they've brought into the prepared shoebox cages. The parent or helper awards each animal a medal (a circus or animal sticker) for its category: most ferocious, rarest, biggest, smallest, most dangerous, fuzziest, etc. Have enough medals and categories so each animal gets an award. Younger children also enjoy playing circus parade with their animals.

Come To The Carnival
Several activities are going on at once, which the guests can join as they prefer. A chart on the wall describes the simple scoring system: 1-10 points = gumdrop, 10-20 points = sticker, 20-30 and up = trinket.

Clowning Around
At one booth or table, the children find a box full of clown clothes and makeup (makeup recipe, page 62) for dressing up as clowns. Have a mirror handy . . . and the camera.

Umbrella Toss
Each player is given ten unshelled peanuts to toss, one at a time, into an open, upside-down umbrella. The sections of the opened umbrella are marked off by numbers taped to the spokes. These tell the player's score. Example: ten peanuts are tossed. Two land in Section 7, one lands in Section 4, six land in Section 2, and the last one lands on the floor. The child's score is 30; the prize is a small trinket.

Hungry Clown
Players stand at a 4-foot distance from a box with a clown face drawn on it and the clown's mouth cut out. Each player is given ten bottle caps or buttons to toss at the clown; the player's score is the number of items that are thrown into the clown's mouth.

Fishing
(See *Pot o' Gold*, "Land of Make Believe," page 27.) Players hold their fishing poles over a curtain or box.

Bop The Pop Can
Players toss a tennis ball at a stack of 6 empty soft drink cans. Each player gets 5 chances; the score is the number of cans knocked over.

Clown-Wheel Race
(See *Tricycle Race*, page 139.)

Tigers Are Out
Hide & Seek, with the players pretending to be tigers.

Back To Your Cages
Players sit in a circle on chairs. Each is given the written name or a picture of a circus animal. One player, the Animal Trainer, walks outside the circle, saying "Calling all tigers ... calling all lions," etc. The players with the names called get up and follow the Animal Trainer. After three or four animals are called, the Trainer claps and calls, "Back to your cages!" The animals rush back to their places, while the Trainer tries to grab one of the empty seats. The person left with no seat is the next Trainer.

REFRESHMENTS
- Circus foods, served from a concession stand or tray (see "Play Ball!", page 114). Popular foods are peanuts, popcorn, Cracker Jacks®, ice cream bars and hot dogs.
- Circus Soda (recipe follows)
- Big Top Dessert (recipe follows)

Cake
- Canopy Cake, made by placing frosted animal crackers around the sides of a frosted layer cake. Top it with a canopy supported by drinking straws. To make the canopy, cut a

circle 8" in diameter from lightweight colored paper. Scallop the edges and turn them down. Tape 6" straws around the circle and a 7" straw in the center. Stand canopy on the frosted cake. "Happy Birthday" can be written on a flag on top of the canopy.
- 3-Ring Cake. Decorate a frosted sheet cake with three bracelets as rings and animal crackers as performers.

FAVORS
- Circus performers from the table decorations
- Prizes won at Carnival
- Balloons

....

Circus Soda

Soda water
¼ cup milk
Ice cream
3 T. flavoring — chocolate syrup, strawberry jam, frozen raspberries, or crushed fresh fruit.

Mix flavoring and milk. Fill each glass to the top with soda water and add a scoop of ice cream. Serve with a straw.

Big Top Dessert

1 package vanilla wafer cookies
1 qt. vanilla ice cream, softened
1 6-oz. can frozen pink lemonade concentrate, thawed

Crush wafers to make crumbs. Set aside. Mix lemonade and ice cream. Sprinkle half the crumbs in individual bowls or 8" square pan. Spoon in ice cream mixture and sprinkle the rest of the crumbs over it. Serve immediately or store in freezer. Serves 10.

Pirate Treasure

Yo, ho, ho, and a bottle of . . . apple juice.

INVITATIONS
- On imitation-parchment paper, or other textured paper, draw a map of the route to the party site. Write the party information below it. Now char-burn the edges: hold a lit match below the paper, going slowly around the edges. This will give it an authentic, antique map appearance. Roll the maps, tie them with twine, and deliver them to the guests.
- Cut construction paper cards into pirate shapes: treasure chest, hat, skull and crossbones, etc.

DECORATIONS
- Form a pirate's cave from a large box or a card table covered with black cloth. Decorate the exterior with a Jolly Roger flag, showing a skull and crossbones. Hang thread inside the cave to represent spider webs, and pin up a picture of a gruesome pirate's face with a dagger clenched in his teeth. Place the cave at the entrance to the party.
- Parent or helper can dress in pirate regalia and greet the guests. Use a plunger for a pegleg, Long John Silver style.
- Hang a Halloween paper skeleton in a corner.
- If guests are Peter Pan fans, place a crocodile and a ticking clock together on a table in the party area.

ACTIVITIES

Treasure Chest

After the guests crawl through the pirate's cave, they encounter a treasure chest: a large painted, decorated box or trunk with a lid. In the box are fake mustaches and beards, hoop earrings, bandanas, sashes, pirate hats, and makeup (recipe follows). Include eyebrow pencils! The pirates outfit themselves in swashbuckler style, drawing scars, mustaches, snarls, etc., with the makeup. For a fearsome look, blacken teeth with tooth blackener from a novelty shop. Make an eye patch from a 1½"-square piece of black felt. A long mirror allows for full appreciation of the effect, and a Polaroid® or other photo of each pirate makes a good souvenir. Decide before the party whether the guests will take their outfits home or put them back in the chest before leaving.

Makeup

Mix 1 tablespoon soft shortening with 2 tablespoons cornstarch. For red makeup, add 2 drops red food coloring. For dark purple (black eye, bruise, mustache), add 1 drop blue, 2 drops red food coloring.

Pirates About

Players divide into two groups in this version of *7-Up*, the pirates and the sailors. The sailors climb into the boat (chairs, lined one behind the other), are all blindfolded, and all begin to row. A pirate sneaks quietly up to the boat and touches one of the blindfolded sailors on the shoulder. The touched sailor stops rowing and stands up. Then another pirate sneaks to the boat and touches another sailor, who also stands up. When all sailors are standing, the parent or helper says, "Sailors beware . . . there are Pirates About!" The sailors' blindfolds are removed, and they guess who touched them. If the guess is correct, the pirate and sailor exchange places; if not, they remain in the same group. The game continues until all have had a chance to be both sailors and pirates, or until time is up.

Pieces of Eight

Each player receives a different map, with pictures, dotted lines, and clues such as, "Walk three steps to the patio bench. Turn left. Walk four steps to the maple tree," etc. At the spot marked "X" on the map, each guest finds a treasure (see Favors). Each player's treasure should be hidden well away from the other treasures.

Dead Man's Cove

Players divide into two teams, "Captain Kidd" and "Blackbeard." Each team has a large ball. Players toss the balls at the opposing team. Anyone hit by a ball must go to "Dead Man's Cove," a designated corner of the room. A player who catches the ball may stay in the game. When all members of one team are in Dead Man's Cove, the game is over.

Buccaneer Buddies

All guests sit in a circle on the floor. The birthday child, who has decided on an insignia or symbol before the party, now explains the ceremony for becoming Buccaneer Buddies. Guests stretch their arms, wrists up, toward the middle of the circle. The birthday child marks each wrist with the symbol chosen (such as an O with an X in the middle), using red water-soluble felt markers. Then all the comrades press their wrists together in the center of the circle and shout, "One For All and All For One!" This is an excellent activity to end the party. The birthday child can also make a potato stamp with a personal insignia.

REFRESHMENTS

- Shish-kebabs on skewers: meatballs, cherry tomatoes, and small potatoes are easy-to-handle choices.
- Hamburgers with crossed bacon strips to represent crossbones.

- Teresa's Pirate Punch (recipe follows)
- Treasure chests (animal cracker or other small boxes) filled with raisins and peanuts
- Oranges (to prevent scurvy!)

Cake
- Treasure Chest. Decorate an ice cream cake or standard square cake as a treasure chest, with jewels of jelly beans and other small, colored candies.

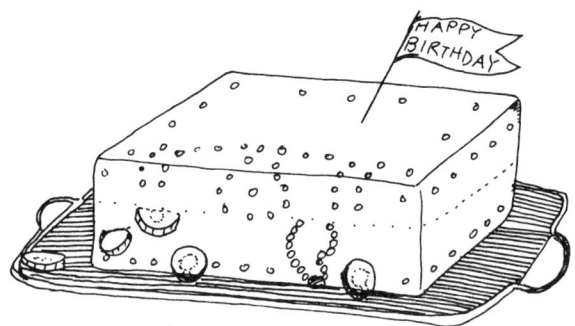

- Pirate Cake. Decorate a flat sheet cake with a pirate scene — green mint frosting tipped with white for waves; plastic or paper boats with Jolly Roger flags; an island of coconut, and a palm tree made from a cut-off straw stapled with green construction paper fronds. Place a treasure chest (watch or small jewelry box) filled with jelly beans in one corner of the scene.

FAVORS
- Pirate accessories
- Items found in *Pieces of Eight* activity: gold-covered chocolate coins, shiny pennies, a miniature Jolly Roger flag, an eyepatch, earrings, a mustache, bags of nuts and candies
- Treasure chests (animal cracker or other small boxes) filled with raisins and peanuts
- Instant photos

. . . .

Teresa's Pirate Punch

½ cup cranberry juice
½ cup orange juice

Pour over ice cubes in glass. Makes one serving.

Gold Doubloon Cookies

Bake a favorite cookie recipe in a 13" x 9" pan, rather than as drop cookies. Cool and cut the cookies into bars or squares. Frost with Creamcheese Frosting.

Creamcheese Frosting

4-oz. package creamcheese, softened
½ lb. powdered sugar
1 t. vanilla
½ cube butter or margarine (4 T.)

Mix until smooth. Excellent frosting for cookies or cakes.

Making Miniatures

Build a house, furnish a castle, design a space station — which is your preference? This party is for the miniature-maker.

INVITATIONS
- Put a picture of a dollhouse (or other building) on a card. Cut shuttered windows that open to reveal the party information inside.
- Use purchased housewarming or open house invitations.
- Make a folded card from construction paper and sketch the birthday child's dollhouse on the front. Write party details inside.

DECORATIONS
- Place the birthday child's dollhouse on a low table or on the floor, with dolls having a party inside.

- Line cardboard boxes of differing shapes and sizes in a row on the floor or low table, forming a street of houses and other buildings. These will be the foundation for the major activity of the party. The boxes should be partially prepared before the party by pasting colorful paper on them. Do the lid separately, as this will be the front of the house and removable. Draw windows and doors; the openings may be cut with a utility knife. Form roofs and chimneys from folded, paper-covered cardboard. This pre-party craftwork is an excellent activity for the birthday child.

ACTIVITIES
Create a House

Each child receives one of the shoeboxes to turn into a dollhouse, firehouse, space station, school, or other building. Examples of supplies they'll need are:

magazines	construction paper
glue	scissors
crayons	clay
felt pens	staples
fabric scraps	egg cartons, cut up
buttons	paper towel cylinders
lace	rick-rack
pipe cleaners	toothpicks
lollipop sticks	spools
plastic lids	cardboard
walnut shells	toothpaste lids
small boxes	

Encourage each child to make more than one item. Have two helpers if 10 children are present. With five or six guests, one helper will do, and with only three children, no extra help is needed.

Furnishing ideas:
Beds
- Use the lid of a small candy box for a headboard, and make legs from folded cardboard.
- Wrap earring or ring boxes with cloth.
- A walnut shell with a scrap of cloth makes a small bed.

Tables
- Turn a small box upside down and glue toothpicks inside the corners for legs.
- Place a circle of lightweight cloth on an empty spool. Put a dab of clay into a toothpaste top and stick strawflowers in it to make a vase.

Stairs
- Accordion-folded paper or cardboard (see Crafts, page 152).

Chairs, sofas, coffee tables
- Use toothpicks or halved popsicle sticks held together with clay.

Mirrors
- Frame purse-size mirrors with yarn. Attach to the walls with glue or clay.

People
- Pipe cleaners, paper and cloth scraps.

Dishes and food
- Cut pictures from magazines or shape items from FIMO, a clay product that bakes hard and lasts forever.

Village Scene
   Those guests who would like to do something different can make a backdrop for the houses and buildings by drawing trees, grass, flowers, etc., as well as other houses, on a large piece of butcher paper or cardboard.

Graham Cracker Houses
   This house-building activity is an alternative to *Create A House*. We don't recommend trying to do both at one party. Each guest is supplied with three large graham crackers, separated to make four sides and a roof (some will break, so have plenty on hand). "Royal Glue" (recipe follows) is used to attach the pieces. Candy canes, gumdrops, and other candies are glued to the outside of the house as windows, doors and decorations. Stack broken cinnamon sticks against the side of the house to make logs, and form a pathway with thin strips of licorice. Add coconut for grass.

Red Light, Green Light
   (See Games, page 139)

Ducks Fly
   (See Games, page 133)

Rescue Relay
   (See Games, page 132)

REFRESHMENTS
- Miniature sandwiches — cut full-sized sandwiches into eighths.
- Vegetables, such as carrots, celery, and cherry tomatoes, sliced in small pieces and served on doll dishes.
- Small baskets filled with candies, nuts, raisins and sunflower seeds.

Cake
- Frosted sheet cake or cupcakes topped with a miniature dollhouse item for each guest.
- Individual cake-houses. Frost a sheet cake and cut it into as many pieces as there are children at the party. Supply licorice ropes, candy, chocolate squares and chips, sprinkles, hard candies, gumdrops, coconut, nuts, and miniature marshmallows so guests can decorate their cake-houses themselves.

FAVORS
- Houses made and decorated by guests
- Graham cracker houses
- Basketful of miniatures from which guests may choose

Royal Glue (edible)

2 cups beaten egg white (about 14 egg whites)
6 cups powdered sugar

Work fast, as the glue hardens rapidly.

Just a few of these ideas are plenty for a successful party.

Rover, Come Over

For a tail-wagging good time, here's a fantastic party to sit up and beg for. To make a cat-lover purr, try the kitty antics that follow the dog party. Or adapt the ideas to other animals — imagine a pig party ... or a fish party!

INVITATIONS
- Cut a card into a dog shape. Write "Rover, come over for a tail-wagging good time."
- Write the invitation on the back of a dog food label.
- Cut a dog cartoon or comic strip from the newspaper. Paste it on a folded card and write the party details inside.

Other animal theme ideas:
- Animal cracker boxes with the party information on a paper inside.
- Cut animal pictures from magazines and paste them on construction paper cards, forming a collage (see Crafts, page 148). This is fun for the birthday child to do.
- Fish food boxes with party information on a rolled paper inside.
- Card shaped as a Cheshire-cat grin, a cat silhouette, or a popular cartoon cat.

DECORATIONS
- Make a doghouse from a large cardboard box with the ends opened to form entrance and exit holes. Label it with a sign reading "Dog House."
- Tape paper paw prints on the floor, leading to the party area.
- Place dog bones, balls, chewing toys, cats, a dog bed, leashes, etc., in the party area.

ACTIVITIES
Into the Dog House

When guests arrive, they crawl on hands and knees into the party room through the dog house (see Decorations). As they crawl through the exit, the birthday child ties dog collars around their necks. Each collar has a typical doggy name: Bowser, Spot, Fido, Rover, etc. The collars are brightly colored strips of felt, 15" x 1½".

Doggie Biscuits

Guests walk on all fours and beg for their supper. They are given doggie biscuits (animal crackers), which they eat from a dish on the floor or have popped into their mouths — with a pat on the head.

Dog Race

The group divides into two relay teams, with everyone on hands and knees. One player at a time from each team must race to the other end of the room and back. The losing team must roll over and play dead.

Obedience School
   Players, on all fours, form a row facing the "trainer" (birthday child, parent or helper). The trainer goes through a series of directions:
   Raise a hand and say, "Sit" (the dogs sit)
   Beckon, saying, "Come" (all walk to the trainer's feet)
   Point forward and say, "Go" (all return to their original places)
   Stretch an arm up and say, "Down" (all lie down)
   Now the trainer goes through the arm signals without the words; the dogs try to follow directions. Players take turns being the trainer. Everyone participating in Obedience School receives a ball.

Find the Bone
   Guests race to find the bones, animal crackers, or dog toys hidden in the party room or yard.

Doggie, Doggie, Who's Got Your Bone?
   (See *Dog & Bone,* Games, page 130.) One player is the dog sitting in the doghouse facing away from the entrance. The other players take turns snatching the bone away.

Red Rover
   (See Games, page 135.)

Dogcatcher
   A variation of Tag, in which It is the Dogcatcher and must tag the scampering dogs.

Animal Race
   Players race their nutshell animals on an incline (see *Nutshell Racers,* Crafts, page 148).

REFRESHMENTS

- Biscuits cut in bone shapes
- Hot dogs, with weiner chunks for legs and head and cheese triangles for ears and tail. Attach pieces with toothpicks.

- Serve granola or bran cereal in empty, clean tin cans labeled "Dog Food."
- Serve cereal, sloppy joes, or stew in dog dishes. Put the guests' names on the dishes.

Cake
- Sheet cake cut in the shape of a dog and frosted with white icing. Trim with chocolate frosting and candies. Use M&Ms® for eyes.
- Sheepdog cake — cover a dog-shaped cake with white frosting and coconut.

FAVORS
Put small favors in empty, clean dog food cans.
- Stuffed animals
- Dog figurines
- Rubber balls
- Dog books
- Animal crackers
- Collars

• • •

Kitty Party Suggestions

DECORATIONS
- Catbed, basket, stacked cans or boxes of food, scratching post, catnip, cat toys, yarn, toy mouse.

ACTIVITIES
The Cheshire Cat Can Make You Grin
All players sit in a circle, unsmiling. The birthday child starts by pointing to one guest who must smile, "wipe" the smile off with one hand, and throw it to another person. Anyone who smiles out of turn is out of the game, and backs up from the circle. Place a time limit on this one.

Cat on the Fence

Players divide into two relay teams and creep like cats, on tiptoes and fingertips, following a chalk or masking tape line. Those who fall must start again. The team that finishes first wins.

REFRESHMENTS
- Tunafish sandwiches
- Ice Cream Meows (recipe follows)

Cake
- Layer cake cut in the shape of a cat or mouse.

. . . .

Ice Cream Meows

Large scoop of ice cream

Chocolate kisses (ears)
Candy/raisins (eyes)
Maraschino cherry (mouth)
Thin licorice strips (whiskers)

Set ice cream on doily and decorate as the head of a cat.

Beyond the Stars

"All systems Go!"

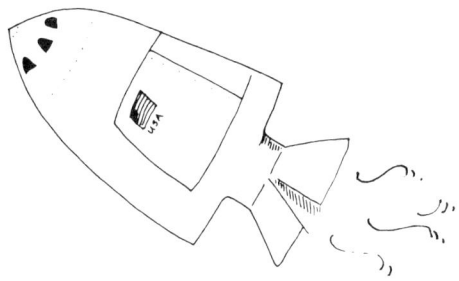

This party is designed as one long adventure-ride through outer space to a strange and far-off galaxy. Make it as elaborate as you wish; the space travel fans will love it. An older brother or sister will enjoy doing it for younger children. For variety, other ideas are provided as alternatives to the space flight.

INVITATIONS
- Cut a card in the shape of a space module, helmet, or rocket ship. Inside the card, write: "T minus Ten and counting for an intergalactic birthday celebration. Blastoff Time and Date:"
- Write the invitation on a page or picture from a coloring book with a space age theme. The birthday child can color the picture or leave it for the guest to color.
- Cut an outline of a space helmet from a folded card. Cover it with aluminum foil, cut an eye space, and tape clear plastic wrap over the hole. Write the invitation inside the card so that some of the wording shows through the plastic. Inside, write: "Beam aboard the birthday space shuttle for a celebration in outer space."

DECORATIONS
- Play records or tapes from current space movies and television programs.
- Hang Christmas lights (the small white ones that twinkle are best) around the ceiling to simulate stars in space.

- Spray-paint or glue glitter on styrofoam balls and hang them on strings from the ceiling.

- Hang silver or white balloons
- Hang paper stars, moons and planets
- Tape posters or space pictures on the walls. They're often available from libraries, science museums, and variety stores.
- On the wall, tape a large cardboard rocket or space map drawn by the birthday child.

ACTIVITIES
Space Ride

To prepare for boarding the spacecraft, each guest makes a helmet from a white paper bag with a hole cut for eyes and nose. The space travelers decorate their bags with crayons, colored pencils, or felt pens.

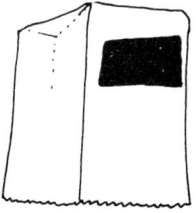 

Now they're ready for the space flight in the "rocket room" which has been prepared in advance. Guests sit back-to-back on the floor in rows, facing tables which have been propped on their sides (card tables, TV trays and picnic tables work best). Each traveler has a large sheet of paper painted with a circle; this is the astronaut's porthole. With crayons, the space travelers will draw the sights they see. If tables aren't available, substitute magazines to provide a firm surface for the 12" x 18" papers.

A description of the ride through space may be read on the

spot (this takes a flair for drama!) or pre-recorded. As the guests take their positions, the reader announces through a megaphone (see Crafts, page 150):

"This is your pilot speaking. Our rocket is on the launching pad, ready for takeoff. Astronauts, check your equipment. Ready for countdown — T minus Ten and counting. 9,8,7,6,5,4,3,2,1 ... Blastoff!"

(Guests imitate the sounds of a spaceship taking off.)

"Our rocket is now lifting from the pad and zooming upward, flattening us into our seats by the force. In just a few minutes after takeoff, we are speeding through space, with no feeling of motion. The earth looks smaller and smaller as we move into interplanetary space. We're now leaving the Milky Way Galaxy and headed for an unexplored planet, Zeroid. Draw what you saw as we left our galaxy."

(Reader pauses for a few breath-catching moments, while the travelers draw space pictures.)

"Watch out, we're headed for a meteor storm. We've been hit! Would Astronauts Gretchen and David go see what damage has been done to our spaceship?"

(The designated astronauts, attached to the spaceship by an imaginary lifeline, pretend to step out into space and check the spaceship, returning to report that everything seems fine.)

"Now we'll continue. It's beautiful out here, seeing stars in faroff galaxies. Now we're headed in to Zeroid. Check your equipment. We'll be sending each one of you off on an exploring mission. Your assignment is to disembark and bring back samples of the life you find there. Ready for landing — retro-rockets firing — and a safe landing on Zeroid. You each have a short time to gather your materials and get back in time for takeoff and the trip home. Be sure your lifelines are secure — and good luck."

(The space travelers leave their seats and go exploring. Throughout the "rocket room" ordinary household objects have been hidden so there is a pile of several items for each guest. Objects might include paper clips, straws, cups, hangers, and pencils. Each guest must gather one pile and return to the spaceship. Then the explorers report on the uses they imagine for these objects. Example: The paper clip is "the Zeroidians' favorite vegetable.")

"Good work, astronauts. Time to get back on board. What's that? It looks like a Zeroidian monster! Quick! Back to the spaceship and prepare for takeoff."

(The astronauts again supply the sounds of takeoff.)

"We're off again. When we're safely on our way, Astronaut Brian will distribute your rations. Please consume them carefully — remember, there is no gravity here to hold your food still."

(The birthday child distributes small plastic bags of treats such as beef jerky, dried fruits, nuts, raisins, and Rocket Fuel Punch [recipe follows] in covered paper cups with straws.)

"There's the Milky Way ahead, approaching fast. We're back in our own galaxy, and there is Earth, straight ahead. Time to fire the retro-rockets. We're slowing — it feels heavy, as we sink into our seats. The command module shield is glowing red-orange as we enter Earth's atmosphere. Down we go to a perfect splashdown! Mission accomplished. Well done, crew!"

The space travelers now disembark to a heroes' welcome and a ticker-tape parade. They march single file from the spaceship to the party table, while the parent or helper throws confetti and parade music plays.

ALTERNATE ACTIVITIES

Photo Space Adventure
   Guests create slides of themselves in space or on alien planets (see *Slide Art,* Crafts, page 149).

Extra-terrestrials
   Guests make extra-terrestrial creatures. When baked in the oven, they shrivel and change shape. (See *Shrinking Shapes,* Crafts, page 153).

Space Shuttle Relay
   (See *Over-Under Relay* or *Hopping to Boston,* Games, page 138).

Time Capsule
   On small (3 x 5) cards, guests write information about themselves to plant in a time capsule. Place all the cards and any other items guests want to include in a plastic bag. Seal it, wrap the bag in foil, and seal that in a metal container. Bury the container and place a marker over it that reads, "To be opened in the Year 2000." Perhaps the friends will have a reunion in that historic year, and dig up the capsule!

REFRESHMENTS
- Space travel foods (see *Space Ride* activity)

Cake
- Cupcakes with small American flags stuck in the frosted tops.
- Angelfood cake, frosted, with a toy rocket in the middle, surrounded by 4th of July sparklers. Rockets are available that actually shoot many feet in the air; if the party is held outdoors or in a spacious area, shoot the rocket off after singing "Happy Birthday."

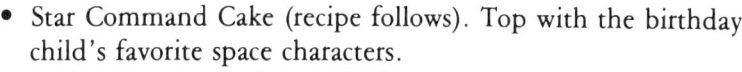

- Star Command Cake (recipe follows). Top with the birthday child's favorite space characters.
- Rocketship sheet cake, made from a 13" x 9" cake iced with white frosting and decorated with the child's name in frosting or licorice. Put all the candles at the bottom. Use red licorice strips for exhaust.

FAVORS
- Space creatures that guests have made (see *Extra-terrestrials* activity)
- Helmets guests have made
- Astronaut/space figures
- Activity books with a space theme
- Posters
- Milky Way® candy bars

Star Command Cake

1 package chocolate cake mix
1 small package chocolate pudding mix, instant-type

Prepare pudding and set aside to cool. Prepare cake batter according to package directions; stir in cooled pudding. Bake in 13" x 9" pan or as cupcakes.

Bingo!

Looking for a fast and easy party to warm up a winter night? Try some of these ideas for a memorable evening of fun and games.

INVITATIONS
- On the front of a folded paper card, paste a playing card from an old deck (the one you never tossed out, even though the two of clubs is missing). Inside, write: "Do not pass Go. Do not collect $200. Do come to my birthday party, and do bring your favorite board game."
- Use a playing card as the invitation; write the party information directly on the card.
- Staple and fold construction paper to make a four-page board game invitation that opens like a booklet. For example:

Page 1: "You're a winner! Move ahead two pages."
Page 2: "1234 Pine Street. Phone 794-3682. Move ahead two pages."
Page 3: "Come to Jane's house Friday, November 5, at 7 p.m. for an evening of games and a birthday celebration. Go back one page."
Page 4: "Bring your favorite board or card game."

- Draw a board game path on a plain square card, with a party detail in each square.

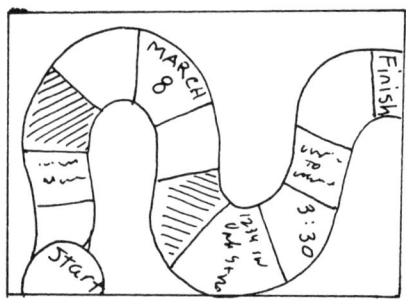

- Make up scorecards for each guest. Example:

Official Scorecard
Rules & Regulations:

1. Date _____
2. Time _____
3. Place _____
4. RSVP _____
5. Bring this scorecard and your favorite board or card game for an evening of fun, celebrating Sandra Wong's birthday.

Scores:

Game #1 _____ Winner_____
Game #2 _____ Winner_____
Game #3 _____ Winner_____

DECORATIONS

- The only decorations needed for this party are several card tables and chairs or low tables with pillows. A fire in the fireplace adds coziness.

ACTIVITIES

Players sit four to a table, with a different game at each table. At the sound of a bell or other signal, they begin playing the games. After 15 or 20 minutes, the signal sounds again and all players rotate to the next table, remaining with the same group of people, but playing another game. They can clear the board and begin the game again, or continue playing where the other group stopped. Players rotate in this way every 20 minutes until every group of four has played every game.

Refreshments are served, and guests then play games of their own preference, choosing from those brought to the party. For a game that involves all the guests in a raucous good time, try *Spoons* (see Games, page 144).

REFRESHMENTS
- Snacks and fingerfoods, served to guests as they play
- Boardwalk Sandwich (recipe follows)
- Popcorn
- Cider or hot chocolate

Cake
- Cake sandwiches, formed by slicing a loaf-shaped cake. Each guest receives two slices, with jelly or frosting between them as filling. Decorate the sandwich as a playing card, using small candy hearts secured with frosting.
- Card cake. Turn a sheet cake into a playing card with the birthday child's age on it. Decorate it with frosting or candies and candles. "Happy Birthday To A Real Winner" may be written on a card and stuck in the cake, rather than done in frosting, if preferred.

FAVORS
- Pocket games (checkers, tic-tac-toe, and cards)
- Deck of cards
- Miniature dice
- Invisible ink game books

Boardwalk Sandwich

4-6 foot loaf of French bread, sliced horizontally (special order — check wholesale bakeries in the Yellow Pages)
Assorted fillings: chicken or tuna salad, cheese, ham, corned beef, etc.

Divide the loaf into four sections and spread each with a different filling. Label the sections and serve. This can also be an activity done by the guests in an assembly line. Adapt to the size of your crowd.

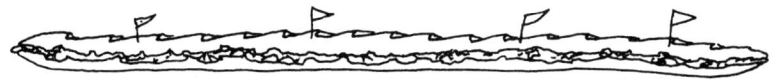

Bon Appetit

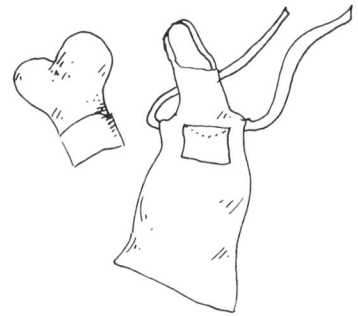

Guests play "chef for a day" in this party that centers around delicious foods prepared, served, and eaten by those attending. Most of the suggestions here are for a pizza party.

INVITATIONS
- Send a folded paper apron, available from party supply stores, or have guests bring paper aprons of their own design. Each guest will receive a prize for the most elaborate, most colorful, most original, etc.
- Use the birthday child's name as the name of the restaurant. Example for a pizza party: Patty's Pizzeria. Other ideas: Johnny's Junk Food Diner, Carol's Creperie, Teresa's Terrible Tacos, Bill's Seven-Flavor Sundae Shop, Loralee's Luaus.
- Send a card cut in the shape of a chef's hat, spoon, or apron.
- Cut pictures of foods from magazines and newspapers to form a collage (see Crafts, page 148). Paste the pictures on the front of a card with the party details inside. This one is fun for the birthday child to do.

DECORATIONS
- Above the party entrance, tape a butcher paper sign with the name of the "restaurant."
- Play Italian "gondola" music.
- Use red and white checked tablecloths and napkins.
- Place a candle in a winebottle.
- Hang posters of Italy.

ACTIVITIES
Wearing the aprons they've brought or been given, guests divide into teams. For a group of eight making pizza:
- Two prepare dough from an instant mix, roll it out, and place it on a baking sheet.
- Two chop tomatoes and grate cheese.
- Two mix a salad of lettuce that has been washed and shredded before the party.
- Two make root beer floats.

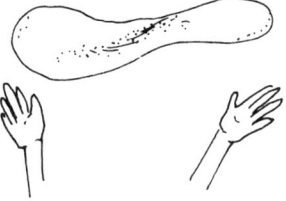

Guests take turns placing items on the pizza dough: tomatoes, cheese, ground beef (cooked before the party), tomato sauce, pepperoni, onions, etc. The pizza is placed in the oven to bake. While it is cooking, guests play *Spoons* (see Games, page 144) and are awarded pizza restaurant coupons as prizes for their apron designs. When the food is ready, guests devour the pizza, salad, and root beer floats in their restaurant setting. Then they head back to the kitchen, where they form an assembly line for making Peanut Butter Bonbons (recipe follows).

FAVORS
- Official chef certificates

Chef For A Day

_____ is hereby given the Golden Spoon Award for outstanding culinary achievements.

_____   _____
  Date   (Signature of birthday child or parent)

- Chef's hats and aprons
- Fast-food restaurant gift certificates for soft drinks, sundaes, etc.

Peanut Butter Bonbons

1 12-oz. package chocolate chips
2 T. paraffin
½ cup butter
1 cup peanut butter
2 cups powdered sugar.

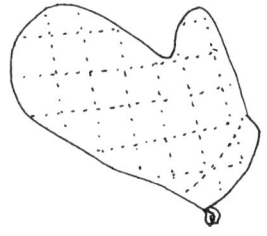

Stir chocolate chips and paraffin in double boiler over hot water (not boiling) until melted. Cream butter, peanut butter, and powdered sugar and form into walnut-sized balls. Dip balls in chocolate mixture. Place on cookie sheet or pie tin and cool in freezer. Keep cool until just before serving; the bonbons will not hold their shape at room temperature.

Recipes for other *Bon Appetit* parties:

Submarine Sandwich
(see Boardwalk Sandwich, "Bingo!", page 88)

5-Cup Salad

1 cup canned crushed pineapple, drained
1 cup mandarin orange sections
1 cup miniature marshmallows
1 cup shredded coconut
1 cup sour cream

Mix well. Serves six.

S'Mores

Graham crackers
Marshmallows
Chocolate bars broken into squares

Place marshmallows on graham crackers and toast them in the oven (10-15 seconds in a microwave). Top each with a chocolate square and another graham cracker.

Hot Fudge Sundae

2 squares melted chocolate
1 can sweetened, condensed milk
½ cup water

Mix ingredients and heat slowly in a double boiler. Pour over vanilla ice cream and serve with whipped cream, maraschino cherries, and nuts.

Ice Cones

Crush ice cubes made from orange juice or lemonade in blender or ice crusher. Put the crushed ice in paper cups. Pour 2 tablespoons fruit juice concentrate over each ice cone.

Milkshakes

1 quart (32 oz.) milk
3 scoops ice cream (chocolate malt, rich strawberry, or other flavors from ice cream specialty shops such as Baskin-Robbins)

Mix in blender. Makes 3-4 small shakes.

Globe-trotting

INVITATIONS

- Create a travel flyer that says: "Experience the thrill of a raft trip on the Congo ... race in a Northland dogsled ... take a camel ride through Egypt. Travel around the world with Tim Brown's Birthday Party Tour Group."
- Have the birthday child cut travel ads from magazines and paste them to the front of a construction paper card.
- Send a postcard of your own town or part of the country, with all the party information written as a note to the guests. Example: "Hi! Having a wonderful time. Why not take a trip and join me here for a birthday party?"
- Cut a construction paper card in the shape of a suitcase; inside place a ticket or token to be brought to the party for a door prize.

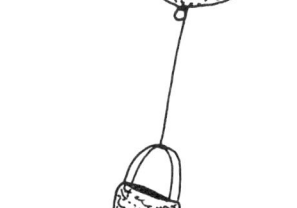

DECORATIONS

- With yarn or string, attach a small paper basket (see Crafts, page 49) to a helium-filled balloon and float it in the party area.
- Put suitcases with travel stickers in a corner of the party room.

- Make a ticket booth from a large cardboard box (see "All Aboard," page 31). Place it at the entry, where the birthday child or helper will collect tickets.
- Hang travel posters or maps on the walls. A used book store is a good source for large maps. With felt pen, or yarn and stick pins, mark the route the travelers will take.
- Display picture books and magazines from the library.

ACTIVITIES
Bon Voyage

The parent or helper, with megaphone in hand (see Crafts, page 150), acts as tour guide, leading the group through this imaginary travel adventure. Extra help is useful in serving the treats.

Players are seated in a row of chairs, which will be their transportation. First they "zoom" to the airport on their motorcycles. Then they board a jet plane for London. During their flight, they are served soft drinks or juice in paper cups. In London, they disembark from the plane and play an English game:

Kickery

While the other players cover their eyes and count to 50, It hides. Then the players spread out to hunt for It. Anyone finding It hides too, in the same place. The last player to discover the hiding place becomes the next It.

Now the travelers board an English double-decker bus, with half the group seated on the chairs and the other half on the floor beside them. Guests are served an English muffin and a cup of tea. Then it's time to climb into a balloon and sail off to Egypt. Guests stand in a close circle; one person unties the rope to release the balloon, and the others throw imaginary sandbags over the side

as the balloon and basket float away. Arriving in Egypt, they descend and climb out to eat a slice of buttered pocket bread and play:

King Tut:
(See *Simon Says,* Games, page 134). The leader says "King Tut Says" instead of "Simon Says," and anyone making a mistake is "mummified" for a count of 10. Place a time limit on the game.

Now the globetrotters take a camel ride by straddling their chairs and facing the backs. They cross the hot, dry desert, finally reaching the Congo River. There they board a raft and pole up the river into the jungle. Deep in the jungle, they go ashore, pick and eat bananas, and play a game of the Congo:

Mubwabwa (Antelope)
Players move outside or to a large area for this game, which is similar to Tag. It tries to catch the others while yelling, "Mubwabwa!" (Moo-bwah-bwah) The first player tagged starts yelling "Mubwabwa!" also, and helps catch the others. The game continues this way until everyone is caught, the last one being the winner.

Back to their chairs for more globetrotting, the guests step into an old-fashioned sailing ship and head for the far Northland. On the way, they adjust the rigging, lower the sails, etc. When they reach the Arctic, they jump ashore where they line up in the snow for a dogsled race.

Dogsled Relay
(see *Wheelbarrow Relay,* Games, page 140.)

After an Ice-Cone break (see Ice Cones recipe, page 92), it's time to head for home. The tour group hops a jet flying home, with a possible stopover in Hawaii for a slice of pineapple.

REFRESHMENTS
- Treats served during trip.
- Sandwich boats — hollowed-out mini-loaves of French bread, filled with egg salad, tuna, or corned beef. Each boat has a sail (made from a straw and paper) labeled with a guest's name.

Cake
- Airplane, boat, bus or balloon shaped cake.
- Sheet cake decorated with a travel scene, such as plastic boats on a blue frosting ocean.
- Home Again Applesauce Cake (recipe follows).

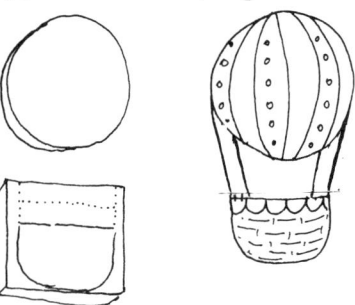

FAVORS
- Miniature suitcases filled with treats of raisins, nuts, or candies.
- Toy planes or boats
- Travel stickers, found in airport and souvenir shops

Home Again Applesauce Cake

2 cups sugar
4 cups apples, peeled and chopped
½ cup vegetable oil
2 eggs, beaten

2 cups flour
2 t. baking soda
1 t. salt
2 t. cinnamon
1 cup chopped nuts

Pour sugar over apples and let stand for ½ hour. Beat other ingredients, stir in sugar and apple mixture, and pour into greased and floured 13" x 9" baking pan. Bake at 350° for 45 minutes. Serve with topping, whipped cream, and a candle on each piece. Serves 8-10.

Topping

½ cup sugar
1 t. vanilla
½ t. salt
2 T. butter
¼ cup milk   Boil until creamy; then pour over cake.

PJ Surprise

Be prepared for lots of giggles at this surprise party with a twist — both birthday child and guests are surprised. The parent is in for some fun, too, at an evening you'll be talking about for months.

INVITATIONS

Guests are invited to a birthday party on a Saturday afternoon. Their parents, however, are secretly told that the real party will be held the Friday evening before. Parents are asked to see that the children are in their pajamas by 8:00 p.m. (this isn't absolutely necessary, but adds to the fun of the party).

At 8:00 the Friday evening before the scheduled party, the parent of the birthday child slips out of the house, drives to the guests' homes, and announces that it is time to leave for the party. The surprise and delight on the faces of the children always makes this a special treat for the adult driving.

The entire group of excited guests then gathers at the birthday child's home to spring the surprise. When the unsuspecting honoree opens the front door, all shout, "Surprise!" and sing "Happy Birthday."

DECORATIONS

A cozy fire in the fireplace is all you need, since this is a surprise party. Balloons and streamers, presumably for the planned Saturday party, add a festive note.

ACTIVITIES

Favorite board games, craft projects, or the following activities are good choices.

Spoons
   (See Games, page 144.)
Detective
   (See Games, page 143.) The parent can be the "thief."
The Perfect Purple Parrot
   (See Games, page 143.)
Bingo and Favor Exchange
   (See Games, page 139.)
Arches
   (See Games, page 129.)

When the party festivities are over, the guests are taken home; or have them bring sleeping bags and make it a slumber party. In the morning, serve breakfast and then deliver the weary, satisfied guests to their homes.

REFRESHMENTS

- Popcorn
- Caramel Corn (recipe follows)
- Donuts. Put a candle in each donut, if cake is not served.
- Brownies (recipe follows)
- Hot chocolate with marshmallows

Cake
- Sheet cake with a frosting rainbow or decorated with items showing the birthday child's interests: horses, sports, hobbies, etc.

FAVORS
- Puzzle books
- Stickers
- Fish fortunes (see "Age of Aquarius," page 126).
- Small pocket games

Caramel Corn

6 quarts popped corn
2 cups butter
2 cups brown sugar

1 t. salt
1 t. vanilla
1 t. baking soda

Mix butter, sugar and salt in saucepan and bring to a boil. Boil five minutes without stirring. Add vanilla and baking soda; stir, and pour mixture over popcorn in baking pan. Bake at 200° for 1 hour, stirring every 15 minutes. Fantastic caramel corn!

Brownies

4 oz. unsweetened chocolate*
⅓ cup shortening & ⅓ cup butter (or all shortening)
1½ cups white sugar
½ cup brown sugar

4 eggs
1 t. vanilla
1⅓ cups flour
1 t. baking powder
1 t. salt

Melt chocolate, shortening, and butter in pan over low heat. Remove from heat; add sugars, eggs, and vanilla. Beat in remaining ingredients, put mixture in greased 13" x 9" baking pan, and bake 25 minutes at 350°. Makes 28 brownies.

*To substitute cocoa: 3 T. cocoa plus 1 T. shortening = 1 oz. chocolate.

Just a few of these ideas are plenty for a successful party.

Knights & Dragons

"In days of old, when knights were bold ..."

Dragons and dungeons, swords and damsels — they're all here in a party that will delight your favorite young knight or lady.

INVITATIONS
- Write the party details on construction paper cut in a sword shape; place the sword in a sheath made of paper glued or stapled on three sides. The sword's handle extends from the sheath, ready to be pulled. On the sheath, write the guest's name. Place the invitation in a long envelope for mailing.

- Make a dragon from accordion-folded green paper (see *Paper Decorations,* Crafts, page 152). Use red paper strips for flames from the dragon's mouth. Write the party details on the dragon.
- Form a card in the shape of a shield, with a coat of arms designed by the birthday child. The coat of arms is divided into four sections; each marked with traditional symbols such as a sword, turret, crown, and helmet; or the birthday child can create personal symbols. Inside the card, write: "You are invited to a birthday gathering of the Knights of The Round Table. Come to the castle on November 2 for a feast and celebration."

DECORATIONS
- Hang black crepe paper streamers or black paper chains in front of the door, to represent an iron gate (portcullis).
- Hang a mural (see *Play Ball!*, page 112) made by the birthday child, showing a crowd watching the jousting.
- Place posters of castles in the party area.

ACTIVITIES
Enter The Castle

As each guest arrives, the court herald (helper) pushes the portcullis aside, opens the door, and announces the arrival with a flourish, through a trumpet. The trumpet is a long cylinder of cardboard with a felt banner or pennant attached. The guests are announced with honorary titles. Examples: "Lady Jennifer of Maple Street," "Sir Steven, Knight of the Realm," "Maid Emily of Sherwood Forest," etc.

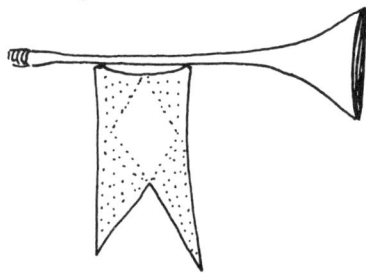

Forge A Sword

Guests make their own swords and sheaths from poster board. Make a few extra swords and sheaths before the party to use as examples and for late arrivals.

Coat Of Arms

This activity is an alternate to *Forge a Sword*. Each guest is given a sheet of poster board cut in the shape of a shield and divided into four sections. In each section, the child draws a picture of an interest or hobby. Staple 1½" × 4" heavy paper on the back of the shield as a handle.

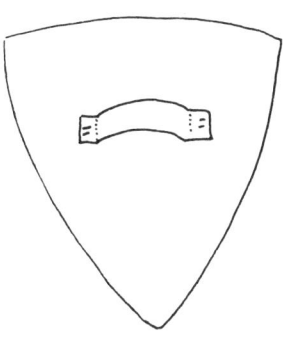

Duchess Headdresses
(See *Hats,* Crafts, page 150.)

Knighthood Quests

The parent or helper announces that, as in days of yore, guests must prove themselves worthy of knighthood by going on a series of quests. The first quest is:

Cross The Moat
Players must slay the crocodiles in the castle moat. With nets, scoops, or a strainer, they capture toy crocodiles floating in a partially filled wading pool or tub. Rubber and plastic crocodiles are available in variety and toy stores. Once captured, the crocodiles are dried and placed in special treasure bags labeled with guests' names. Then the players move on to the second quest.

Jousting
Each knight-errant must joust with the magic troll, charging toward it and knocking it down twice with a sword. The troll is a weighted, inflatable punching bag doll that bounces back when knocked over.

Slay The Dragon
Each guest must slay a dragon and return with its remains. Before the party, green balloons are blown up, and a piece of a map leading to the dungeon (see *Into The Dungeon* quest) is placed inside each balloon. Then the balloons are taped to the inside wall of a closet. Knights and Ladies take turns using the special sword — King Arthur's Excalibur — to pop the balloons. This plastic or heavy cardboard sword has a pushpin attached to the end.

Into The Dungeon
Players assemble the map pieces found when slaying the dragons to guide them to the dungeon for their final

quest. When the map is assembled and glued or taped to a piece of paper, they follow its directions to the dungeon. Along the way, they encounter cobwebs (soft strings hung from the ceiling) and hear water dripping, moans, and rattling chains. In a corner of a semi-darkened room is a large, black-painted box. This is the dungeon. Each guest must reach into the opening in the box and pull out whatever is touched first. Items touched are treats or small prizes to be taken home.

Their quests accomplished, guests are knighted by the parent. They kneel and are touched on their shoulders with the sword, while the parent says, "I dub thee Sir Jason, Knight of the Realm," "Julia, Princess of Buckingham," etc.

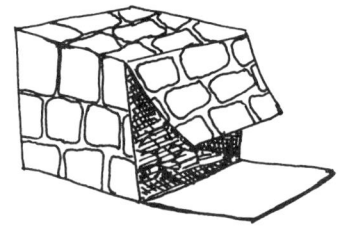

Merlin's Magic

If someone who knows magic tricks is available for the party, the magician wears a Merlin-style cone hat and robe, and dazzles the guests with sleight-of-hand tricks. To find a magician, check the Yellow Pages under "Magicians."

Drawbridge

Players form two teams, the White Knights and the Black Knights, separated by a line or masking tape on the floor. Merlin (a helper or the birthday child), dressed in a robe and decorated cone hat, waves a paper or stick wand and calls, "Drawbridge down!" The Black Knights then cross the line and chase the White Knights, trying to tag them. After 5-10 seconds, Merlin says, "Drawbridge up!" The Black Knights must return to their side of the line, along with any White Knights tagged. They have now become Black Knights and must help tag. When all have been caught and become Black Knights, the game starts again with the teams reversed. This activity requires outdoor space, a basement, or large party area.

REFRESHMENTS

- They didn't use forks in King Arthur's day — so serve fingerfood such as bologna slices, cheese, fruit, or chicken drumsticks.
- Grape juice in goblets

Cake
- Cupcakes topped with marshmallows. Poke a sword into each marshmallow, representing Excalibur, the sword King Arthur pulled from the stone. Swords may be plastic swizzle sticks, available in novelty shops, or handmade from toothpicks and paper.

- Shield cake. Cut a 13" x 9" cake in the shape of a shield. Frost in bright bands of color.

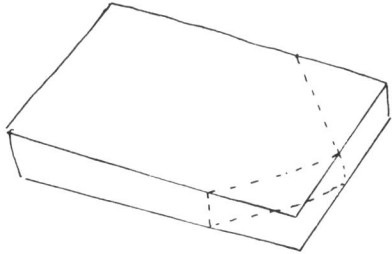

- Castle cake. Cut a 13" x 9" cake into three sections. Use inverted ice cream cones as turrets and chocolate squares for windows and entrance.
- Merlin's Magic Cake (recipe follows).

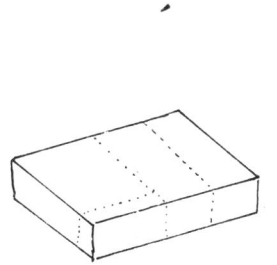

FAVORS
- Swords and sheaths
- Crocodiles from moat
- Shields with coats of arms
- Duchess headdresses
- Plastic miniature knights on horseback
- Merlin's Magic Kit. Include a wand, pointed hat, and magic potion (canned fruit juice).

Merlin's Magic Cake

1½ cups flour
1 cup sugar
1 t. baking soda
3 T. cocoa
1 t. salt

1 t. vanilla
1 T. vinegar
5 T. oil or melted shortening
1 cup cold water

Sift flour, sugar, soda, cocoa and salt into an ungreased 8" x 8" pan. Make three dents in the mixture and pour vanilla in one, vinegar in another, and oil in the third. Pour water gradually over all and stir until smooth. Bake 25 minutes in a 325° oven.

Hobo Heaven

INVITATIONS
- With red felt pen, write the party invitation on a page from the Jobs Wanted section of the newspaper. Fold the paper, tie a cloth bandana around it, and deliver. Guests bring the bandana to the party; it will be filled with treats, attached to a stick, and taken home as a "bindlestick."
- Write the invitation on the back of a wrapper from a tin can.
- Send a hobo shack card.

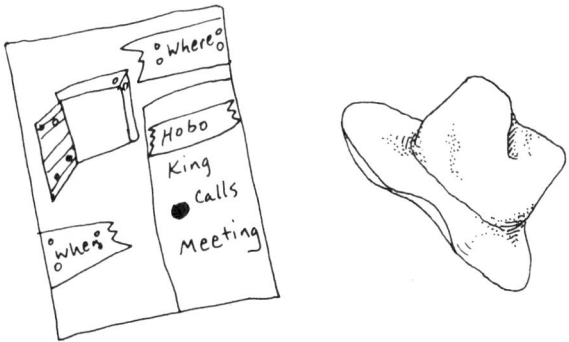

- Cut a card in the shape of an old boot, a patch, a battered hat, or a boxcar. Inside, write: "To all hoboes. Catch a fast freight to Jerry's house for a birthday party."
- Give guests hobo nicknames: Iron Mike, Railroad Joe, Bumtown Billy, So Long Sal, Rough and Ready Betty, etc. Ask them to come dressed as hoboes.

DECORATIONS
- Use chunks of wood, wooden crates, or campstools for seats and overturned boxes for tables. Bring in tree branches for more atmosphere.

- Place paper flowers in tin cans.
- Label a cardboard box shanty (see "Home On The Range," page 44) with a sign: "Bums Only."
- Use newspapers for tablecloths and weed-filled catsup bottles for vases.
- Create a campfire: 1) red tissue paper or cloth over a flashlight or 2) red light bulb in a small lamp surrounded with sticks and twigs.
- Place a scruffy toy dog by the campfire.

ACTIVITIES

Hobo Faces

As guests enter, they make up their faces to look like hoboes. (For ideas and makeup, see "Pirate Treasure," page 62). They add to their costumes by choosing old, ragged clothes from a box; then they're given large Tootsie Rolls® as "stogies." This is a good time for picture-taking and a parade.

King Of The Hoboes

As King of the Hoboes, the birthday child uses an old, rickety chair as a throne and wears royal garb: a beach towel robe, wooden spoon scepter, and an upside-down pot as a crown. He sits on the throne to open presents. The King is also the leader of the parade.

Police And Conductor

Two players are the Police Officer and the Conductor. They try to catch the Bums in a game of Tag. When caught, the Bums are placed in Jail (use cardboard box shanty), but they can escape after counting to 50.

Snitch The Pie

Hoboes take turns sneaking quietly to a table in the kitchen, where a row of cherry tarts is set out. They attempt to snitch one and get it back to the campfire before being "noticed" by the cook.

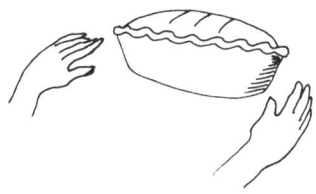

What's In The Hobo Bag?

Hoboes take turns reaching into a large paper bag and writing on a paper what they think they touched. The bag contains such items as a stick, a can label, rock, toy boxcar, tin mug, empty match book, bent spoon, and closed pocket knife.

Broom Relay

The hoboes line up in two rows. The person at the front of each row has a broom and a balloon. At a signal to start, that player sweeps the balloon to a line marked on the other side of the room, and then sweeps it back and hands the broom to the next player. The first team to have all its members out and back wins the game.

Hop A Freight

The guests play Hopscotch (see Games, page 136), but instead of numbers in the Hopscotch squares, names of railroad lines are written. Players jump from one RR line to another. Some railroad names to use are: Great Northern, B&O, AT & Santa Fe; So. Pacific; Amtrak.

Campfire Tales

Parent or helper tells stories around the campfire.

REFRESHMENTS

- Rubber Chicken Punch. Place a rubber or plastic chicken in a serving pot full of punch (recipe follows). For effect, be sure the chicken's legs dangle over the edge of the pot. Guests dip a ladle into the pot and serve their own punch into tin cups.
- Hobo Stew (see Gypsy Goulash, page 127). Serve with chunks of French bread.
- Hot dogs, cooked over an open fire, in the fireplace, or precooked and served around a fake fire.
- S'mores (see *Bon Appetit*, page 92)

- Cherry Tarts (see *Snitch The Pie* activity). Place canned cherry pie filling in small pie crusts and bake according to directions on filling label.

Cake
- Cut a sheet cake into boxcar shapes. Frost them and decorate as railroad freight cars. Use Lifesavers for wheels and thin black licorice for a track.

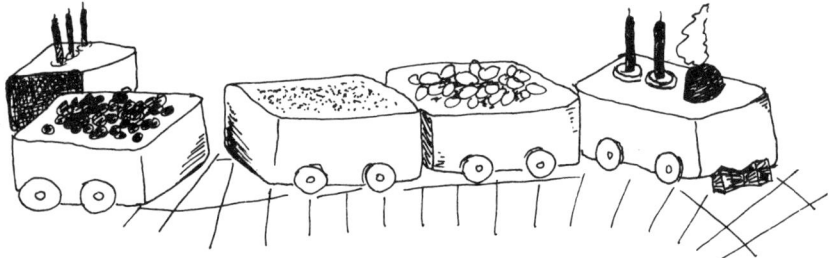

FAVORS
- Tootsie Rolls®
- Boxcars decorated and filled with goodies (see Crafts, page 149)

- Bindlesticks
- Photos of guests in costume

....

Rubber Chicken Punch

1 6-oz can frozen concentrated fruit-juice punch, thawed
2 cups apple juice
1 cup water
⅓ cup lime or lemon juice
¼ cup sugar (if desired)

Mix all ingredients until sugar dissolves. Serves 6. Add one rubber chicken.

Play Ball!

Here's an exciting event for the youngster who eats and sleeps sports. These suggestions are geared to the baseball addict, but they can easily be adapted to other favorite sports.

INVITATIONS
- Hand-deliver a plastic baseball which has the party information written on it with felt pen.
- Cut paper into an invitation shaped like a baseball, mitt, bat, or ticket to a ballgame. If it's a ticket, it is brought to the party as admission to "the game."
- From the newspaper sports page or a magazine, cut pictures of ballplayers and paste them on folded cards. Write the party details inside.
- For a party with friends who often play ball together, request that guests come as their favorite baseball players. Each should wear a hat, shirt, or tag identifying the player and team. The guests should be prepared to answer a number of questions, such as: "Where are you from? What is your team? What position do you play? What is your league batting average? Do you throw/hit left or righthanded? Write the answers to these questions on a card and bring them to the party. You will be interviewed!"

DECORATIONS
- Place a ticket booth at the door (see page 31). Decorate the booth with red, white and blue bunting (crepe paper) or banners. The ticket booth can double as a concession stand at refreshment time.
- Draw a grandstand on butcher paper and tape it to the wall. Guests can color it in later as one of the party activities.

- Hang baseball posters.
- Have the birthday child write baseball statistics in large print on butcher paper, and hang this in the party area.

ACTIVITIES
Trivia Quiz

As guests arrive, each is given a sports-facts booklet (found in grocery and variety stores) or a sports page from the newspaper. Players sit in a circle. One asks a sports question that is answered in the book or paper. The others guess the answer. The first to answer correctly then asks the next question. Put a time limit on this one.

Balloon Ball
(See *Call Ball*, Games, page 136.)

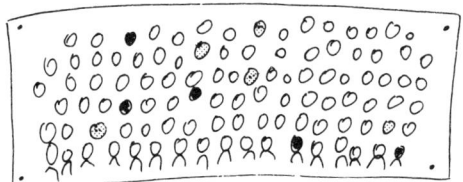

Harold Mosell Interview

Each player is interviewed by "Harold Mosell" (parent or helper), who holds a microphone. A second helper takes instant photos. An actual audio or video recording of the interview adds greatly to the fun of this activity, but it isn't necessary. A fake microphone can be made from a cardboard cylinder, string, and a tennis ball attached to the cylinder with strong glue. Mosell says: "Good evening, sports fans, this is Harold Mosell at _____ Stadium. I am here with _____ of the _____. _____, what are your feelings about the upcoming season? What is your batting average? What are the difficulties of your position? Who is the toughest player you have come up against?" ...

and so on, asking the questions that were listed on the invitation. After the interviews, the players listen to themselves on the tape, if they were recorded. Keep each interview short, so every player gets a turn.

Great Moments in Sports
Guests listen to radio broadcasts of great moments such as Hank Aaron's record-breaking home run. Records are available at most libraries. The local sports team may also have promotional films that are available to the public.

Promotional Contest
A tray of items such as shaving lotion, hair spray, and soap is displayed; each player chooses one item. One at a time, they stand before the rest and endorse the product. The best performance, as judged by the other guests, wins a baseball card or gum.

Locker Room
Guests play *Bag of Clothes* (see Games, page 136), using sports tote bags filled with jerseys, sweat socks, visors or caps, and other sports clothes.

Air Ball
(see Games, page 141.)

Baseball Cards
Guests trade baseball cards or make their own by attaching instant photos (from the *Harold Mosell Interview*) to 5x8 cards. They write their own farfetched statistics on the backs of the cards.

Bubble Gum Contest
Players are given bubble gum, and each tries to blow the biggest bubble.

Guests may be taken to watch a baseball game, or celebrate the party with their own game at a nearby playground.

REFRESHMENTS
- Peanuts, ice cream bars, popcorn, ice cream sandwiches, and hot dogs served from a concession tray. Make the tray from a long, flat box. Attach lengths of heavy yarn to the sides of the box and tie them around the concessionaire's neck. The treats can be served midway through the party as part of the ongoing festivities.

- Meatloaf, mashed potatoes, and milk served family-style at a "Training Table."
- Energizer Punch, served in a "Relief Pitcher." (Recipe follows.)
- Vanilla ice cream scoops, decorated with chocolate frosting squeezed from tubes to look like the seams of a baseball. These can be prepared in advance and stored in the freezer.

Cake
- Baseball Diamond. Decorate a square cake as a baseball diamond, with bases of candy and miniature plastic ballplayers.
- Pennant Cake. Cut a sheet cake in the shape of a pennant. Frost and decorate with candy canes and the words: "The Winner, Jason Dunn."

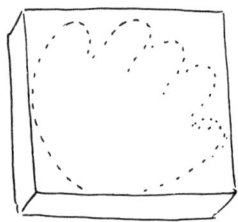 

- Baseball Mitt. Bake brownie mix (or see Brownies recipe, page 99) in an 8" square pan, and cut the cake into a baseball mitt shape. Frost it with chocolate icing. In the center of the mitt, place a baseball (top half of a cupcake, frosted in white).

FAVORS
- Personal baseball cards from *Baseball Cards* activity
- Baseball caps from novelty shops
- Bubble gum
- Purchased baseball cards
- Big League Chew® — shredded bubble gum

A memorable favor for the birthday child is a regulation baseball autographed by everyone present.

....

Energizer Punch

3 quarts lime sherbet, softened
4 quarts ginger ale or 7-Up

Mix and pour. Serves 20.

Japanese Tea

*Otanjo Omedeto!**

INVITATIONS
- Make a paper or cloth-covered card shaped as a teacup, Japanese lantern, fan, or flower.
- Send a Japanese fan or folded paper bird with the party information written on it.
- Form a paper into a fan shape with accordion folds. Write the party details on the folds; the recipient must open the fan to read it.

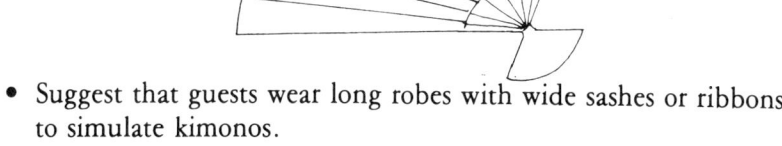

- Suggest that guests wear long robes with wide sashes or ribbons to simulate kimonos.
- Explain in the invitation that each guest is to bring to the party a wish written on a small piece of paper. It will be tied to a "wishing tree" and read aloud.

*Happy Birthday!

DECORATIONS
- Play records or tapes of traditional Japanese music, available at the public library.
- Hang carp kites at the party entrance. (See Crafts, page 152.)
- Place paper lanterns and parasols about the room.
- Hang wind chimes.

ACTIVITIES
Wishing Tree
As guests arrive, they tie their wish-papers to the wishing tree — a bush in the yard or, indoors, a branch stuck in clay. Then they remove their shoes and enter the party area. Midway through the party, guests pick their own or another wish and read it aloud. Telling the wish aloud helps it come true!

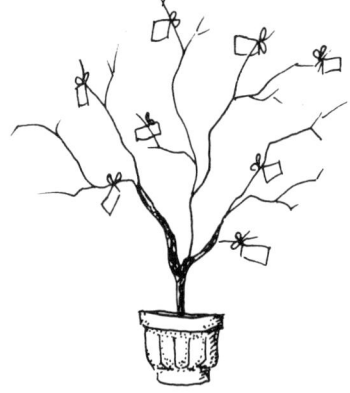

Ocha No Kai (Japanese Tea)
In a room or corner decorated with a simple flower arrangement done by the birthday child, a tea set is placed on the floor or low table. No chairs are used. Guests sit or kneel on the floor in front of their hostess and are given hot, wet washcloths to freshen their hands. The hostess wears a robe and tabi, or white Japanese socks. At the sound of a bell or other musical signal, the hostess bows deeply to the guests. Into each cup, she pours Japanese green tea that has been

steeping in the pot. She then serves a rice cookie to each person. When her guests have finished drinking their tea and have eaten their cookies, the hostess makes a low bow and guides them to the next activity.

Shoe Scramble

(See Games, page 131.) Since shoes were removed when the guests entered, this is a fitting activity to follow the tea.

Jan, Ken, Po (Stone, Paper, Scissors)

Players sit on the floor facing each other in pairs. In unison, the two facing each other hold out their hands and say, "Stone, Paper, Scissors." At Stone, one hand is in a fist; at Paper, it is flat; at Scissors, index and middle fingers are extended. As Scissors is said, the player may use the stone, paper or scissors symbol. If one player ends with Stone and the other with Scissors, Stone wins that round, since Paper covers Stone, Scissors cut Paper, and Stone crushes Scissors. This game can be played over and over again, so a time limit should be set.

Jan, Ken, Po Relay

Players divide into two teams and sit at opposite corners of the room. The first person on one team meets the first person on the other team in the center of the room, and they play one round of "Jan, Ken, Po" (see above game). The loser joins the team in the winner's corner, and the next person on the loser's team goes to the center to play the game. When all players on both teams are in one corner, the game is over.

Hanakago (Flower Basket)

Players sit in chairs or on floor cushions in a large circle. Each is assigned the name of a flower. There is one less seat than there are players. The extra player (It) calls the names of two of the flowers. Those two players rush to trade seats. While they are running, It tries to get one of the empty seats. The person left out is the next It, who calls two more flower names. The game continues until all flowers have been called or a time limit is reached.

Guess The Rice
    Players guess how many grains of rice are in a rice-filled jar. The closest guess wins. Before the party, the birthday child can count the rice grains in one tablespoon and then count the number of spoonfuls required to fill the jar. This avoids having to count every grain as it is placed in the jar.

Lantern Maker
    (See *Lanterns,* Crafts, page 153.)

Japanese Bath
    If a whirlpool or hot tub is available, request that guests bring their swimsuits and towels and take a dip in the tub as a refreshing substitute for the traditional Japanese bath.

REFRESHMENTS
- Rice, to be eaten with chopsticks, served in small bowls
- Stir-fried vegetables with slivers of meat
- Japanese noodles
- Mandarin oranges
- Mandarin sherbet
- Rice cookies

Cake
- Individual cupcakes, each with a tiny paper parasol
- Sheet cake with "Happy Birthday" written in Japanese characters on the frosting.

ハーピー　バースデー

FAVORS
- Paper lanterns made in *Lantern Maker* activity
- Fans
- Parasols
- Oriental souvenirs from Oriental import shops

Sapporo Icebox Squares

18 coconut cookies, crushed
1 cup whipped cream
1 t. vanilla
1 pint vanilla ice cream, softened
1 pint raspberry sherbet, softened
1 pint lime sherbet, softened

Mix cookie crumbs, whipped cream, and vanilla. Spread half of mixture in bottom of 13" x 9" pan. Spoon ice cream over mixture, smooth, and place in freezer for a few minutes to set. Spread raspberry sherbet over ice cream and freeze to set. Spoon lime sherbet over all, top with remaining crumb mixture, and freeze. Serves 8. Stand a small paper parasol in each serving.

Just a few of these ideas are plenty for a successful party.

Age of Aquarius

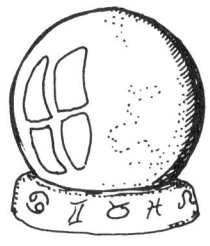

Charting your course by the stars ... palm-reading ... Ouija boards ... crystal balls ... gather them all into one party, where guests will have a good time celebrating and looking into their futures. This is most effective as an evening event, when shadows and flickering candles lend mystery.

INVITATIONS
- Copy the birthday child's zodiac sign onto the front of a folded card. Write: "It's in the stars — your horoscope says a good time lies ahead." Put party information inside the card.
- Outline the birthday child's hand on paper. Fill in the major palm lines and write the party details on the lines.

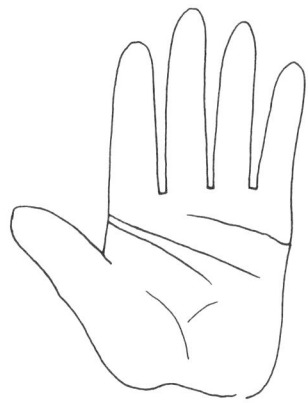

- Draw a crystal ball on a card, with the words: "The Great Swami knows all and tells all. Look into the crystal ball." Inside the card, write: "You will soon attend a birthday celebration honoring Pamela. Much merriment is predicted."
- Save several days' worth of horoscope sections from the newspaper or magazines, and paste them on invitations.

DECORATIONS
- Hang a banner over the entry, reading: "Enter The Year of The Tiger" (for the year's correct animal, see Birthday Symbols, page 155).
- Under the banner, hang a curtain of beads or streamers.
- Tape zodiac posters and maps of the solar system on the walls.
- On a large sheet of paper, draw a hand with the palm lines labeled.
- Burn incense.
- Dim the lights and place vigil lights or low candles on the table.
- Hang paper stars and a crescent moon on strings.
- Put red night lights in wall sockets.
- Place dry ice in corners of the room. Use care in handling dry ice.
- Hang twinkle lights and angel hair for a misty effect.

ACTIVITIES
Find Your Future

In different parts of the room, or in separate rooms, guests take turns at various ongoing activities:

Palm-reading.

Guests compare their own palms with the major lines of the palm (see Decorations). Books with more detail are open on a table nearby.

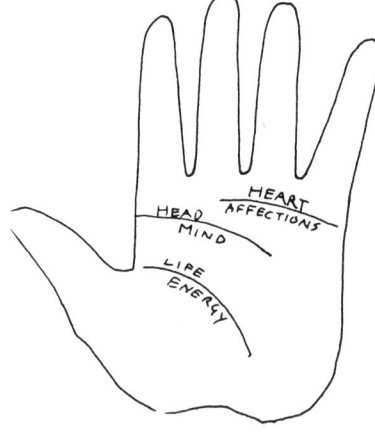

Ouija Board.
The game is set on a cardtable; the parent or helper explains how to play. Place a time limit for each group of two players.
Horoscope.
A zodiac chart of all twelve sun signs is set up at this table, along with books that describe the characteristics of each sun sign. (See Birthday Symbols, page 155, for simplified version).
Fortune Teller.
A stranger to the party guests (or someone well disguised) has been briefed with information about each guest. She sits in a darkened room or in a closet with her crystal ball (a fishbowl with a vigil light inside). She's dressed as a gypsy fortune teller, in a long skirt and shawl, hoop earrings, and jangly jewelry. One at a time, the guests, who have been given silver paper stars beforehand, go to meet the fortune teller. She says, "Cross my palm with silver and I will tell your fortune." The guest gives her a silver star and she gazes into the crystal ball, muttering that "the picture seems to be clearing." The fortune teller then reveals something about the child's hobbies, vacations, favorite foods, sports, etc. Of course the comments should be on the light side. After a few minutes of hocus-pocus she sits back and says, "The picture is fading. Come back when you have more silver."

Alternate Activities
Pick A Fortune
Guests draw paper fortunes from a bowl. Samples: "A journey over the sea and through the jungle awaits you." "A tall, dark, mysterious stranger will cross your path." "You will get something new within a week."
Read The Palm.
Guests are given drawings of a hand outline. They mark the lines they see on their own palms onto the paper hands. The papers are then mixed together in a pile, and each person

pulls one out and guesses whose hand it is by matching each other's hands to the drawings.

Twenty Years From Now

The birthday child prepares in advance for this activity by cutting magazine and newspaper pictures in each of seven categories: wife, husband, children, occupation, house, car, and pets. The fun will be enhanced if the pictures are outrageous and farfetched. The pictures are placed face down in labeled boxes. Each player takes one page from each box, without looking at the picture, and places the papers into an envelope with the guest's name on it. Players then sit in a circle and pull their pictures from the envelopes to see what they'll be doing 20 years from now. The combinations can be hilarious. If desired, the pictures may be mixed up again and the game repeated, or the pictures pasted on a sheet of construction paper and taken home.

REFRESHMENTS

- Gypsy Goulash (recipe follows). Serve with chunks of dark bread.

Cake

- Sheet or layer cake decorated with the birthday child's zodiac sign.
- Frosted sheet cake with various small objects placed so each guest receives one on a piece of cake. When everyone has been served, announce the symbolic meaning of each object. Coin: early wealth. Button: will always be in style. Ring: early love and marriage. Thimble: good at crafts. Marble: good in sports. Toy airplane: will travel frequently.

FAVORS

- Palm drawings guests have made.
- "Fish Fortunes" — paper fish that curl in your palm, revealing your emotions.
- Envelopes with pictures of the future (see *Twenty Years From Now* activity).
- Symbolic items from cake.
- Books of guessing games.

Sources for more information:
Age of Aquarius: You & Astrology
   Franklyn M. Branley, Thomas Y. Crowell, NY 1979
Holding Hands; The Complete Guide to Palmistry
   Peggy Thomson, Prentice-Hall, Inc., Englewood Cliffs, NJ 1974
The Hand Book
   Elizabeth Brenner, Celestial Arts, Millbrae, CA 1980

. . . .

Gypsy Goulash

4 lbs. boneless beef chuck, cut in cubes	caraway seeds
6 T. cooking oil	⅔ cup cold water
2 14-oz. cans beef broth	6 T. flour
2 cups chopped onion	1 t. salt
2 small green peppers, cut in strips	½ t. pepper
4 T. tomato paste	dairy sour cream
1 T. paprika	

Using a large saucepan, brown beef cubes in oil. Add broth, onion, green pepper, tomato paste, paprika, caraway seeds, salt and pepper. Blend cold water and flour; stir into beef mixture. Simmer, covered, until meat is tender (1½ hours). Stir occasionally. Serve over cooked noodles and garnish with sour cream.

Games

Starting with games for the very young, on up to those enjoyed by all ages, here's a full range of choices for birthday party fun.

Animals' Birthday
   Players sit in a circle, with one blindfolded guest in the center. The parent or helper whispers the name of an animal to each child. When the blindfolded player says, "Happy Birthday, Pig," or "Happy Birthday, Cow," etc., the child designated as the animal mentioned makes the appropriate sound: "Moo," "oink," "meow," etc. The blindfolded player guesses the name of the child making the animal sound. The players may prefer to close their eyes rather than be blindfolded.

Arches
   All players form a circle, and two make an arch by facing each other with upraised hands. As the music plays, the other children walk through the arch. When the music stops, the two players forming the arch try to catch the person marching through. When two players have been caught, they form an arch at a different place in the circle, and the children march through both arches. When two more are caught, they form a third arch, and so on until one player is left: the winner.

Puzzles
   Puzzle games can be made by cutting up a picture book and pasting the pages on heavy cardboard. Cut a puzzle into six sections for young children, and more for the older ones. Players assemble the sections to make a whole picture.

Ring On The String

Players sit in a circle with their hands on string that has a ring on it. The string has been tied together at the ends. The children pass the ring from lap to lap while one player walks around the outside of the circle and tries to guess who has the ring.

Charlie Over The Water

Players form a circle and join hands. One player, "Charlie," stands in the center of the circle. Players walk or skip in a circle, chanting:

> "Charlie over the water,
> Charlie over the sea,
> Charlie caught a blackbird
> But he can't catch me!"

As they say "me," the players squat quickly, hands touching the ground. Charlie tries to tag a player before the player gets into a squatting position. The child tagged becomes the new Charlie in the center of the circle. Suggestions:

Don't let the game drag. If Charlie is slow in tagging, choose another player to help. If the group is large, two or three children can be Charlies.

Dog & Bone

One player (It) sits on a chair facing away from the other players. A bone (spoon or toy) is placed under It's chair. The parent or helper quietly points to a player in the group, who sneaks up and takes the bone. Everyone then pretends to be holding the bone and says, "Doggie, doggie, where's your bone? Someone's come and taken it home." It turns around and has four guesses as to who took the bone. If It does not guess correctly, the other players identify the thief. The parent or helper points to another It, and the game continues.

Who's Got The Button?

Players sit in a circle. One child goes from person to person, carrying a button or item related to the party theme, and pretends to slip the item into each person's hands (everyone's hands are folded). The child with the button drops it into one person's hands, continues pretending for a few more, and then stops, saying, "Button Button, Who's got the button?" Players try to guess who has the button; the one who guesses it correctly is It for the next time.

Snicklefritz

Players stand facing their partners. One extra person acts as caller. The caller says, "Back to Back," and the partners turn so their backs touch; "Side to Side," and the partners touch sides; "Hand to Hand," "Ear to Ear," "Ankle to Ankle," and "Bottom to Bottom." The calls are given in any order, and at some unexpected point the caller shouts, "Snicklefritz!" and all must change partners. The caller, too, tries to find a partner. The person left without a partner becomes the next caller.

Who's Missing?

While It's eyes are closed, one child leaves the room. Then, with eyes open, It guesses who has gone. If It is right, the player who left is It next time. If the guess is wrong, It's eyes are closed again and the missing person returns. Then It gets three guesses as to who has returned. If the guesses are all incorrect, the other players provide three clues and then the answer. This is best in a large group.

Sticker Fun

Purchase stickers with different smells such as peanut butter, strawberry, pine needles, bubble gum, and cinnamon. These are very popular with younger children and can be used in several ways.

1. Guests sit in a circle, each with a paper bag containing six smelly stickers. Closing their eyes, they pull the stickers from the bag and try to identify the odors.
2. One guest, blindfolded, walks around the circle of guests and attempts to identify the smell of the sticker held in the hand of each child. Everyone claps whenever a correct guess is made.
3. Guests trade stickers they receive. This requires a variety of stickers divided among the children. They may trade the stickers they receive until a timer or buzzer sounds; then trading time is up. Another trading session may be held before the party is over.

Who Is Knocking At My Door?
   Players face It, whose back is turned. At a signal, one child walks up behind It and knocks on the floor. It says, "Who is knocking at my door?" The knocker answers, in a disguised voice, "It is I." It has three guesses to identify who is knocking at the door. If It guesses correctly, another player becomes the knocker. If It cannot guess, then the knocker becomes It.

Rescue Relay
   Divide the group into two teams standing in relay rows behind a starting line. The first player on each team stands on the goal and faces the team across the room. At a signal, this player runs back to the team, grasps the hand of the second player, and runs back to the goal line. The second player then runs back to the team, grasps the hand of the third player, and returns to the goal. Each player on the team is taken to the goal line in this manner by the previous player, until all have been "rescued" and are in relay rows behind the goal line. The team finishing first wins the relay.

Run For Your Supper
   One player is It; the others form a circle. It goes around the outside of the circle and, stopping between any two players, says, "Run for your supper!" The two players turn away from It and run in opposite directions around the circle, each trying to get back to the other's empty space. The last one back is It, and the game repeats.

What's That?
   Players are seated facing the same direction and given paper and pencils. Items are dropped one at a time behind their backs, and they identify what they hear. Suggestions: spoon, quarter, book, pencil, spool, ping-pong ball, keys, shoe, comb. Records with sounds are available in many libraries.

What's The Prize?
   Wrap a small prize in several boxes and layers of paper. While music plays, the package is passed in a circle from guest to guest, but may be unwrapped only when the music is stopped. The player who finally pulls the prize from the box may keep it.

Huckleberry Beanstalk

While players are out of the room, a small object is hidden. The players return and hunt for it. A player who finds the object does not point it out but takes a seat and says, "Huckleberry Beanstalk!" This continues until all players have found the object.

Adapt to the theme of the party by changing the call words:
- "Hi-yo Silver" or "Ride 'em Cowboy" for "Home on the Range"
- "Shiver Me Timbers" for "Pirate Treasure"
- "Strike three, you're out," for "Play Ball!"

Suggestions:
- The object should be different from other items in the room (a saucepan lid in the living room, for example)
- Hide the object no higher than child-eye level
- Let the child who first spies the hidden object hide it next time the game is played, or be It for the next game.
- If it is not convenient for all players to leave the room, have them cover their eyes while the object is hidden.

Search

Each guest is given a container to hold the objects found, and at a signal goes off in search of items hidden in the area. Animal crackers, jelly beans, Lifesavers, peanuts, play money, jacks, beads or small items relating to the party's theme are examples of treasure to find. To avoid a free-for-all, assign a particular corner or area of the room to each child.

Brownies and Fairies

Players divide into two groups, the Brownies and the Fairies. Goal lines are marked across both ends of the play area, about 40 feet apart, if possible, with the Brownies on one line and the Fairies on the other. All the Brownies turn their backs to the Fairies who, upon a silent signal, begin to sneak quietly toward the Brownies. When they are within 10 or 15 feet, the parent or helper calls, "The Fairies are coming!" and the Brownies turn and chase the Fairies back to their own goal line. Any Fairy tagged before reaching the goal line becomes a Brownie and goes back with that group. Next time around, the Fairies turn their backs and the Brownies sneak up on them and are chased.

Ducks Fly

One player is It. The others form a circle and begin to walk. It stands in the center of the circle and says, "Horses fly, cows fly, dogs fly, birds fly." When a creature that flies is named, players go through the motions of flying by flapping their arms. When something that does not fly is named, players continue walking but do not "fly." Those who fly when they shouldn't or don't fly when they should go to the center of the circle and watch.

For a quieter game, guests may sit in a circle rather than walk.

Pin The Tail On The Donkey

Hang a target on the wall and supply the guests with paper tails to pin on the donkey. Each child in turn is blindfolded, spun around three times, and sent in the direction of the target. The one who pins a tail closes to the target wins. Variations are endless and are adaptable to almost any theme. Note: Sometimes younger children do not like to be blindfolded. Have them close their eyes and ignore the peeking.

Musical Chairs

Line chairs in a single row, facing in alternating directions, or line them in a double row, back to back. With one player more than the number of chairs, the guests walk to music around the chairs; when the music stops, all must sit down. The player left without a chair is out of the game, and joins the adult in clapping to the music. One chair is removed and the march and music begin again. The game continues until there are two players and one chair left; the one who gets the final chair is the winner.

Simon Says

Guests stand in a row and obey the instructions of the leader standing before them: "Right arm up," "left arm up," "bend your knees," "hop," etc. The directions must be followed *only* when the leader begins each by saying, "Simon Says." If that phrase is omitted, the players do not follow the instruction. The winner is the child who can follow the leader without being tricked into an action that did not begin with "Simon Says." That person becomes the next Simon.

Gossip

Players sit in a circle. Behind one hand, so no one can hear, the leader whispers a brief sentence such as, "The moon is full and the witches are out," into the ear of the person on the right.

That person whispers the same sentence to the next person, and so on around the circle until the last person says it aloud to the leader. The leader then tells the original sentence. The changes can be surprising.

Squirrel And Nut

Players sit in a circle, their right hands open and behind their backs. One player is the squirrel, who walks behind the others and drops the nut (or any small article) into one of the open hands. That player jumps up and tries to tag the squirrel, who reaches safety by running around the circle and taking the place left by the one with the nut. If the squirrel is tagged, the squirrel must try again; if not, the one with the nut becomes the next squirrel.

Silver Ball Toss

Guests take turns tossing a silver ball (a piece of crumpled aluminum foil wrapped around a peanut) toward a group of five saucepans placed at one end of the room. Each guest gets five tosses; the one who gets the silver ball into the pans most often is given the peanut inside the ball.

Safety Tag

Any tag game is "safety tag" if there is a position the players can assume that will keep them safe from being tagged. In "Squat Tag" players are safe from tagging when they assume squatting, or deep-knee-bend, positions. In "Ankle Tag," a player is safe by grabbing and holding both ankles. Suggestions: If the group is large, select more than one It. If the game seems slow, tell the players they can only have five seconds in the safe position.

Red Rover

Players divide into two teams, facing each other in lines. Team One calls for a runner: "Red Rover, Red Rover, send Franklin right over." The player called from Team Two runs toward Team One's line and tries to break through their locked hands. If the runner succeeds in breaking through, a child from Team One is chosen to join Team Two. Runners who cannot break through must join that team. The two lines take turns calling "Red Rover" until all players are on one side or the time limit is up.

Warmer, Warmer

One child leaves the room and another hides a theme-related object. The absent player returns and begins looking for the hidden object, while the rest say, "Warm, warm, warm as toast," and "Cold, cold, cold wind blow" as the child gets closer or more distant. "Hot, hot, you're on the dot" means the object is right next to the searcher. Players take turns at being the searcher.

Hopscotch

Squares numbered 1 to 10 are drawn on cement with chalk. (They may also be scratched in dirt with a stick or marked on a large sheet of butcher paper.) A player starts by tossing a penny, button, rock or other small item into Square #1. The player, staying within the marked lines, hops over that square and into the next one, bends over, and picks up the rock — all while balancing on one foot. The player then hops into each of the remaining squares, using two feet where squares are side by side. At Square #10, the player turns around and hops back to #1. Now the rock is thrown into Square #2 and the process repeated until a mistake is made. If the rock lands in the wrong square or on the line; if the player steps on a line; or if the player uses two feet where one is the rule — it's the next player's turn. The winner is the player who makes tosses and hops all the way to Square #10 and back.

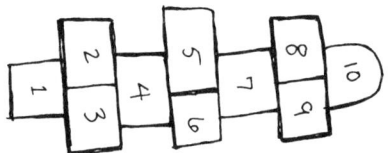

Bag of Clothes

Players stand in a circle. While music plays, a bag full of clothes that fit the theme of the party is passed from one person to the next. When the music stops, the person caught with the bag must put on one article of the clothing. The game continues until the bag is empty.

Call Ball

Players form a circle, with one child in the center, who tosses the ball high while calling the name of a child in the circle. That player attempts to catch the ball before it bounces more than once. If the player catches the ball, that player changes places with the child in the center and becomes the ball-tosser. If the ball is not caught, however, the first ball-tosser continues to toss and call until a player is successful in catching the ball.

Suggestions:
- Use a volleyball, any large, soft ball, or a balloon.
- To add challenge to the game, gradually increase the size of the circle, and have the players catch the ball before it bounces.

Shoe Scramble

Guests sit on the floor in a circle, take off their shoes, and pile them in the middle. At a signal, they rush to find and put on their own shoes. The first one finished wins.

Penny Toss

Each guest holds five pennies or buttons. Players take turns tossing the items, one at a time, toward three bowls 5 feet away. The bowls, placed in a line, should have wide tops and deep sides. Pennies that go into the closest bowl win a raisin for the player; in the middle bowl, a sticker; and in the farthest bowl, a trinket.

Popcorn Relay

Players take turns picking up as many pieces of popcorn (flat chocolate candies may substitute) as they can get on a table knife and carrying them across the room to a bowl. Only one hand may be used, and any spilled popcorn must be left. If the group is small, each guest may have more than one turn. Players may eat the popcorn or candies that make it into the bowl.

Animal Relay

The group divides into two teams, standing in relay rows. Players must progress to a goal line and back to the team, using some manner of animal walk. Variations may be: 1) Donkey walk, traveling on all fours to the goal, imitating the donkey's kick and bray; 2) crab walk, crawling on all fours sideways, with the face up; 3) lame dog, walking on two hands and one foot; 4) bear walk, moving on all fours, with feet going outside of hands; 5) duck walk, squatting and waddling on two feet.

Postcard Puzzle

Cut postcards that relate to the party's theme into puzzle shapes. Put the pieces of each postcard into a separate envelope, and put the envelopes in a hat. Each guest reaches into the hat, pulls out an envelope, and at a given signal begins to arrange the puzzle pieces. When the postcards are complete, they are replaced in the envelopes and saved to be taken home. Keep the game going by trading envelopes.

Over-Under Relay

The group divides into two teams, standing in relay rows. The first player on each team holds a ball. At a signal, the first player passes the ball over her head to the second player, who passes it between his legs to the third. The ball is passed (not thrown) "over and under" the whole length of the row. The last player to receive the ball runs forward to the front of the row and starts it moving again. This is continued until the players are back in their original lineup, with the ball in the hands of the original first player. The team finishing first wins.

Hopping to Boston

Players stand in two lines, behind a starting point. At the signal to start, the first player in each line hops on one foot to a mark on the floor 10 feet away. The player touches the mark with a hand, while balancing on one foot, then hops back to the line and tags the next player, who follows the same procedure. If a raised foot touches the ground at any time, the player must start again. The team that is first to get all its members back to the starting line is the winner.

Bingo

Guests play bingo with purchased or homemade cards. Items that fit the theme of the party are used as markers. Examples: Coffee beans for "Hobo Heaven," fake gold coins or pennies for "Pirate Treasure," and gummed stars for "Age of Aquarius."

Favor Exchange

At the beginning of the party, each guest picks a wrapped box with a favor inside. When a game is played, the winning player or team exchanges the unopened favor with another guest. This works well with *Bingo, Penny Toss, Pin The Tail On The Donkey,* and memory games.

Red Light, Green Light

Players stand on a starting line. It, back turned toward the rest, is on a goal line at the other end of the play area. It calls, "Green Light!" and the other players begin running toward the goal. It counts aloud to five, then says, "Red Light!" and turns to face the runners. All players must stop running at "Red Light!" If It sees a player moving, that player is sent back to the starting line. Each player tries to be the first to touch It at the goal line. The one who succeeds becomes the next It, and the game is repeated.

Tricycle Race

This game is fun for all ages. On tractors, tricycles, wagons and scooters, guests race from a starting point along a clearly marked course to the finish line. (Walk the course the first time through.) At the halfway point, such as the end of the block or the big maple tree, racers must pull over to the "refueling station" and grab half a cup of fruit juice before taking off again. Helpers hand out the juice cups, start the race, and end it with a checkered flag. A wreath of flowers for the winner and treats for all participants adds a finishing touch.

Wheelbarrow Race
　　Players are divided into two teams. Each has a starting point and a finish line about 30 feet away. With the first player's hands on the starting mark, and legs held by the second player, the two race for the finish line, where they reverse positions and return to the starting line. Players Three and Four on each team report the procedure, and so on through all members of the team.

Mind Teaser
　　A number of everyday objects are placed on a tray and covered with a cloth. The players sit in a circle with the tray in the middle. It is uncovered and the players watch it for a few moments; then the tray is covered again, and the guests write as many objects as they can remember. The child with the longest, most accurate list gets to be leader for the next activity.

Blindman's Bluff
　　One player is blindfolded, while the others move into a wide circle and stand still. The blindfolded child is spun three times and then reaches out, trying to touch one of the people in the circle. When someone is caught and identified, the blindfold comes off and the recognized person becomes the "blindman."

Code Messages

On a large piece of butcher paper, write the alphabet. Under each letter place a number or a symbol.

A	B	C	D	A	B	C	D
1	2	3	4	@	%	*	)

Guests write messages to each other using the code.

Air Ball

Players sit in 2 rows, about 4 feet apart, with a piece of string or tape midway between the rows as a net. The center player on one team holds a balloon and blows to start it moving. Players then keep the balloon in the air, blowing it or hitting it with their heads or feet, but not their hands. When the balloon hits the ground on one side of the string or tape, the opposing team gets one point. If it lands directly on the string, neither side scores. The first side to reach 10 points wins. This is a very active game. If you have the space, it can be played standing up in volley ball fashion.

Lip Reading

Seated in a circle on the floor or at a table, one player silently mouths a 3 or 4 word sentence toward another player. The second player has three chances to guess the sentence. The correct answer gives that person a turn at "silent talk." The parent or helper should start the game to demonstrate how distinctly the lips must move to form words that can be understood.

Suggested sentences: "You are funny." "There's food on your nose." "Make a funny face." "Look at the ceiling." "Look at the floor." "Pick up your fork." "Wink at (another guest)."

No clues are allowed except the moving lips.

Wear Is It?

At the beginning of the party, guests are separately and secretly given small items to wear in plain sight. A paper clip on a belt, a pencil behind the ear, and a ribbon around a wrist are examples. Later in the party, guests are told that all are wearing items that do not belong to them; within ten minutes, they are to find the items and list them, as well as the person wearing each one.

Ping Pong Blow

Players kneel by two lines of tape placed three feet apart. A ping pong ball or marshmallow is placed between the lines of tape. Players try to blow the ball over the lines of tape.

Squirrels In Trees

Players divide into groups of three; each player is numbered "One," "Two," or "Three." Numbers One and Two join both hands to form a tree. Number Three is the squirrel, who stands in the tree formed by the other two players. One or more extra players are squirrels without trees. When the parent or helper calls, "Squirrels run!" all the squirrels run from their tree to another tree, and while they are running, the extra squirrels try to get into a tree. Only one squirrel is allowed in a tree, and someone is always left without a tree with each change. When all the trees are full, the signal is repeated and the game continues. After a short period of play, each squirrel changes places with one of the players forming the tree, so everyone has a chance to be a squirrel.

Stunts

Players draw numbers written on slips of paper from a hat. Each must perform a stunt that corresponds to the number drawn. Examples:
1. Gallop and neigh like a horse.
2. You are an extra-terrestrial exploring a kitchen.
3. Walk the plank.
4. You are a camel, racing across the desert.

Marbles In Cups

Players are given 5 to 10 marbles each and take turns rolling or shooting them into paper cups set on their sides about 6 feet away.

Raisin Relay

Guests are divided into teams, and every player is given a dish with five raisins and a toothpick or small spoon. The first player on the team feeds raisins to the second player, using the toothpick, to feed them one at a time. The second player then feeds the third, and so on until the last player is fed and runs to the front of the team to feed the first player. The team that finishes first is the winner.

The Perfect Purple Parrot

One player begins a story in which the words all begin with the same letter. The second player continues the story, using the same letters, and so on until the story is completed, everyone has had a turn, or there are no more ideas. Example: Player #1: "The perfect purple parrot ..." Player #2: "paraded politely ..." Player #3: "On the pink polished poopdeck ..." Player #4: "He puffed his pale, pointed pipe ..." etc.

Who Am I?

Slips of paper or cards, each with the name of a famous person, are pinned to the backs of all players. They must guess "who am I?" by asking the others questions that have a yes or no answer. (Am I American? Am I a movie star? etc.) As soon as a player guesses the correct name, the paper is removed and that player helps someone else. The game continues until all names have been guessed.

Whistle-Soda Cracker

Players divide into two teams, standing an equal distance from a table that holds a plate of soda crackers. At a signal, the first person on each team runs to the table, eats a cracker, and whistles. The whistle is the signal for the next person on the team to get a cracker, eat it and whistle. The first team to finish wins. (Expect cracker crumbs on the floor after this game!)

Detective

The day before the party, one guest is asked to visit the home of the birthday child, wearing the clothes and shoes to be worn at the party. While visiting, the guest:
- Outlines a footprint on paper and hides it in the party area;
- Leaves a thread or bit of fuzz from the clothing worn;
- Leaves a bit of hair in a conspicuous spot;
- Hides a personal item, preferably with an initial, such as a keychain, Mother's picture, scarf, etc.

Then a major item such as a picture or a candlestick is removed from the room. The stage is set for the mystery.

At the party the next day, it is announced that a robbery has taken place — a valuable item has been stolen. Everyone must help identify the thief, using five clues. All guests (including the one who helped set the scene) are given pads of paper, pencils, and for the full effect, magnifying glasses and bubble pipes. They are told that the first clue is that the robber is someone in the room.

Then the detectives start searching for other clues. When one of the four remaining clues is found, it is placed in an envelope, and when all are found, the group uses them to figure out the mystery person. The one guest who knows pretends to work along with the rest.

When they think they know the answer, the detectives announce their findings. The parent or helper then opens an envelope which contains the name of the robber, and tells the detectives if they are right or wrong.

The "guilty" party must then pay for the crime by serving the cupcakes or snack.

Spoons

Players form a circle on the floor, with a group of spoons in the center, handles out. There should be one less than the number of players — 9 spoons for 10 players, for example. Each player is dealt 4 cards. The object of the game is to get 4 of a kind by passing, discarding, and drawing cards. The dealer starts by passing one or two cards to the person on the left and picking up one or two from the deck, to equal four. The person on the dealer's left may keep the cards received or pass them on to the next player and draw more from the deck. People pick up and discard as fast as possible, trying to get four of a kind. The first player to succeed takes a spoon. Others who see this grab spoons, too. The one left without a spoon is assigned the letter S, and the cards are reshuffled and dealt again for the next hand. If the same person is left out when all the spoons are taken, the letter P is assigned. The game continues until one person spells out the word SPOON by being last to reach for a spoon 5 times. That player is out, one spoon is removed from the circle, and the game continues. The last one left in the circle is the winner. Here's an extra twist — anyone can pretend to reach for a spoon at any time. Of course the others rush to grab one. Any player taking a spoon before it's "legal" is assigned a letter.

Old Standbys

Crafts

Sculpting
  Supply clay, aprons and newspapers, for the guests to create items relating to the party's theme.

Sand Color
  Each guest is given crayons and pieces of sandpaper. Pictures and designs are drawn and colored directly on the sandpaper to create bright, rough-textured pictures.

Pudding Pictures
  Guests are supplied with an assortment of puddings, canned or made from instant mixes in different flavors. Add food colors to vanilla. On shiny shelf paper, the children make finger-lickin' good designs. Aprons or old clothes are essential for this one.

Painted Cookies
  Roll chilled cookie dough and cut shapes. Place cookies on baking sheet and paint with egg-yolk paint (recipe follows), using fine watercolor brushes. Bake and remove cookies from oven before they are browned, to keep the colors clear.

Egg-yolk Paint

2 egg yolks
1 t. water
liquid food coloring

Mix egg yolks and water. Divide into 4 small dishes and stir a different food coloring into each. Use enough color to make bright tints.

Paper Dolls
  Fold paper accordion-style. Cut shape desired, making sure to not cut the folded edge.

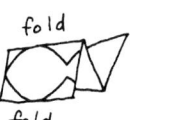

Baker's Clay
   Mix together 1 cup flour, ½ cup salt, 2 teaspoons cream of tartar, 1 cup water, 2 tablespoons vegetable oil, and food coloring in color desired. Bake dough at 350° for 3 minutes. It will fall upon spoon when done. Knead dough until pliable and cool.

Paint-A-Sheet
   With permanent marking pen or water colors, paint designs that fit the party's theme on a white sheet. Use the sheet as a tablecloth for the party.

Collage
   Cut out several pictures from magazines and newspapers. Paste them on a sheet of construction paper. Yarn, string, ribbon, and other trims may be added.

Finger Puppets
   Cut the fingers from old gloves and decorate them with marking pens, yarn, and scraps; or trace a pattern by placing your hand on paper and drawing the outline. Cut two sides of fabric for each puppet, sew them together, and decorate.

Magnetic Puppet Show
   Cut out paper figures and glue a paper clip to each one. On a sheet of cardboard, draw a background scene. Hold small magnets behind the cardboard, and the puppets will move where the magnet goes.

Sock Puppets
   Draw, sew, or glue faces on the feet of old socks. Use yarn, scraps, buttons, and trims. Pulled over a hand, a sock makes a quick puppet.

Nutshell Racers
   Glue a marble inside an empty half-walnut shell. Add a mouse, turtle, or rabbit head of construction paper. Use scraps, fabric, and trims to add features. On a slanted board, race the creatures; the marbles make them slide. These are good party favors.

Mobiles
There are several ways to make mobiles. Tie strings or fishing line to the objects that will hang on the mobile. Attach the strings at different levels to wires, sticks, or cardboard. Umbrella spokes and hangers are ideas for unusual mobiles.

Photo Adventure
Ask guests to bring photos of themselves in action (ones they won't mind cutting up) to the party. Each guest cuts a photo and glues it to a sheet of paper and then draws or colors in an adventurous setting. The photo could also be glued to a magazine picture or poster.

Slide Art
Wipe the picture from a 35-mm slide with a cotton swab dipped in household bleach. The film will turn blue, then become clear. Draw on the clear slide with colored marking pens and acrylic paint. Have a slide show through a viewer, or project the pictures on the wall.

Placemat Prints
Roll a ball of modeling clay the size of a walnut and flatten one side. Make a design on the clay by making an impression with a nail or pencil. Brush the clay with ink or paint, then press it on a sheet of paper cut to placemat size. Napkins and paper cups can also be printed with these designs.

Boxcar-Basket
On a 3-inch square of sturdy paper, snip each corner toward the center. Fold on dotted lines, as shown, and bring cut corners together. Cut a 3½ " × ¼ " strip of paper for a handle. Glue,

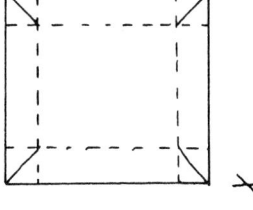
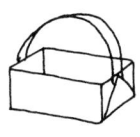

staple, or tape corners and handle together to form a box shape. For a boxcar, cut a 3″ × 5″ rectangle, fold as for the basket, and glue paper circles or Lifesavers on the sides for wheels.

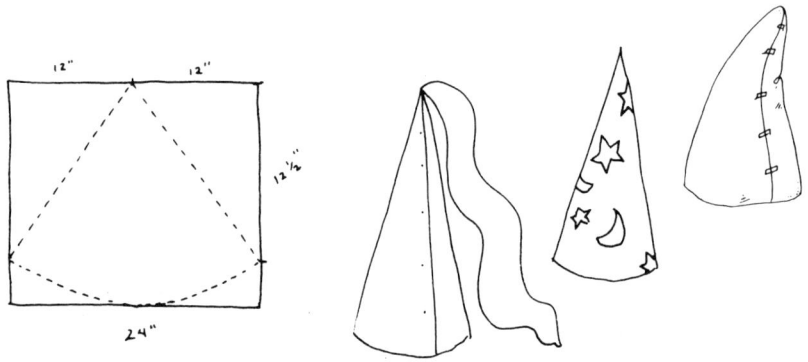

Hats

Duchess headdress, Merlin's magic hat, elf hat, or megaphone. From an 18″ × 24″ sheet of newsprint (found in art supply stores), cut on dotted lines as shown. Form a cone. Staple or tape to fit each guest's head. Use hair pins to help secure headgear. For megaphone, leave an open space at the tip. Duchess headdress: attach strips of crepe paper or filmy fabric. Merlins' hat: Decorate with gummed stars. Elf hat: use green paper.

Indian headband.

Cut a 2″ × 24″ strip from a sheet of newsprint. Cut 8″ feathers from construction paper. After guests color and decorate their feathers and headbands, staple feathers to handband, form a circle from it, and staple the ends to fit the child's head.

Engineer's hat.

Cut a 2" × 24" strip from a sheet of newsprint or construction paper. Cut a hat outline from the rest of the paper as shown, and staple to the strip. Write the guest's name on the hat and staple or tape the ends of the strip together.

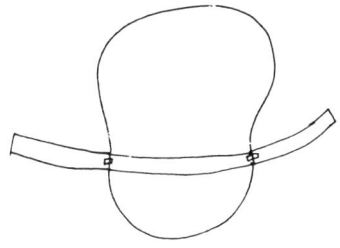

Top hat.

Cut a 12" circle from black construction paper. Cut a 6" circle from the center, forming the hat's brim. From another piece of black paper, roll a cylinder 8" high and 6" in diameter. Cut ½" slits around one end. Push this end through the brim and tape or glue the cut edges to the underside.

Bonnet

Cut the center from a paper dinner plate and staple a paper soup bowl to the plate. Decorate with straw flowers, ribbons, yarn and bows. Punch holes on the sides of the plate to allow for yarn ties.

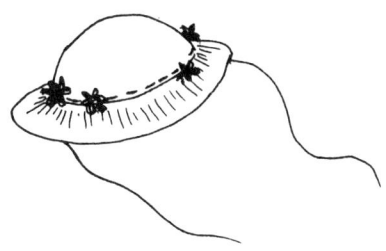

Tiara or Fairy Crown
   Using white or gold construction paper, cut a 4" × 24" strip with points in the center. Decorate with colored marking pens and costume jewelry or sequins attached with glue. Staple or tape the ends together to fit each child's head.

Paper Decorations
- Curl paper strips with scissors or roll them around pencils. (hair and decorations)
- Pleat paper strips into folds. (stairs and dragon)
- Fold paper strips so they stand up. (animals, people, and flowers)
- Fringe and curl paper strips. (eyelashes, curtains, and hair)

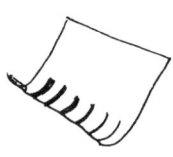

Japanese Kite
   Fold a newspaper sheet in half lengthwise and draw a fish shape. Cut the fish out, but do not cut on the fold. Open the fish and draw gills, scales, and other fish features. To strengthen the fish's mouth, where the string will be attached, fold the mouth edge under twice, about ¼" each turn, and glue it down. Tape a long string around the edge. Fold the fish in half and glue the edges closed, except for the mouth. Stuff the fish with small pieces of newspaper.

Spinners

Cut three cardboard circles and glue them together. Poke 2 holes, ¼" apart, through the middle of the spinner. Decorate the spinner with crayon designs. Thread a yard-long string through one hole and back through the second hole. Tie the string ends together in a knot. Move the spinner to the center of the loop, wind up the strings, and keep the spinner going by spreading arms, then bringing them together.

Shrinking Shapes

Make a design with marking pens on a plastic lid, egg carton, or meat tray. Cut out the plastic shape and punch a hole in the upper part. Place it on a piece of aluminum foil that has been crumpled and then opened. Put the plastic in a preheated 350-400° oven for 1 to 2 minutes and watch it shrink and curl. Remove from the oven and flatten it with a book. Push an 18" length of yarn through the hole and tie to make a necklace. This also makes bracelets, key chains, birthday cake ornaments, ID tags, and invitations.

Lanterns

Each guest is given a piece of colored construction paper, 9" × 4". The piece is folded in half lengthwise and cut in narrow fringe-like strips, with a ½-inch border left uncut on the side opposite the fold. The paper is unfolded and its narrow edged are pasted or stapled together. To add a handle, staple a strip of paper 6 inches long to the lantern.

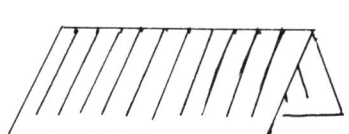

Birthday Symbols

ZODIAC SUN SIGNS

January 20-February 19   AQUARIUS   *The Water Bearer*
Lucky, changeable, likes to lead the way and help others. Enjoys being different. Likes puzzles and riddles.

February 20-March 20   PISCES   *The Fish*
Deep, quick to change from happy to sad, quiet. Likes arts and sports.

March 21-April 19   ARIES   *The Ram*
Friendly, a leader, likes new ideas and sports.

April 20-May 20   TAURUS   *The Bull*
Steady and strong, likes working alone, is slow to anger. Healthy and good with finances.

May 21-June 20   GEMINI   *The Twins*
Changeable, has many interests, does several things at once. Active, likes sports.

June 21-July 22   CANCER   *The Crab*
Curious, stubborn, a collector. Likes water-related sports.

July 21-August 22   LEO   *The Lion*
Risk-taker, likes adventure, decoration and clothes. Good actor and leader.

August 23-September 22   VIRGO   *The Virgin*
Musical, a reader, likes plays, jokes, a few good friends. A good student.

September 23-October 23   LIBRA   *The Scales*
Justice-seeker, weigher and balancer. Sees all sides to arguments. Likes team sports, fish, animals, and designing clothes.

October 24-November 22   SCORPIO   *The Scorpion*
Determined, hard worker, energetic, curious. Makes decisions easily. Likes sports that compete with the clock or record.

November 23-December 21   SAGITTARIUS   *The Archer*
Outgoing, sharp, likes people, always seems to have money. Active in clubs. Likes traveling with others.

December 22-January 19   CAPRICORN   *The Goat*
Eager, ambitious, practical. May work after school to earn money. Hobbies are useful ones, such as repairing.

CHINESE ZODIAC CALENDAR

YEAR OF THE BOAR *1947-59-71-83-95*
People born in the Year of the Boar have strength, fortitude and honesty. Their friends are for life. They are loyal, knowledgeable, well-informed, and quick-tempered. They are affectionate and kind with loved ones and work hard at solving conflicts.

YEAR OF THE RAT *1936-48-60-72-84*
People born in the Year of the Rat are noted for their charm and looks. They work hard, have high goals, and like to acquire possessions. Basically thrifty, they are generous mostly with the people they love. Rat Year people are easily angered, but don't show it outwardly. Their ambitions are big and they are honest, open, and successful. They love to gossip.

YEAR OF THE OX *1937-49-61-73-85*
People born in the Year of the Ox are patient, speak little, and inspire confidence. They have fierce tempers, are mentally and physically alert, and dexterous to the point of genius. They're easygoing but stubborn and they hate to fail.

YEAR OF THE TIGER *1938-50-62-74-86*
Tiger people are sensitive, deep thinkers, and sympathetic. They are short-tempered and may conflict with older people or those in authority. They have trouble making decisions. They are courageous and powerful.

YEAR OF THE RABBIT *1939-51-63-75-87*
Rabbit people are articulate, talented and ambitious. They are admired and trusted, financially lucky, tactful and kind. They are clever in business, conscientious, and never back out of an agreement.

YEAR OF THE DRAGON *1940-52-64-76-88*
Year of the Dragon people are healthy, stubborn, honest, and brave. They are energetic, sensitive and sincere. They tend to be softhearted and are capable.

YEAR OF THE SNAKE *1941-53-65-77-89*
Snake people speak little and have deep wisdom. They are financially fortunate and try to help others. They prefer to rely on themselves and hate to fail. They appear calm but underneath have intense feelings. They are usually good looking.

YEAR OF THE HORSE *1942-54-66-78-90*
People born in the Year of the Horse are popular. They're cheerful and sometimes talk too much. Good with their hands, they are talented, wise, skillful with money, and showy in dress or manner.

They like entertainment and large crowds where the action is. They are extremely independent.

YEAR OF THE SHEEP   *1943-55-67-79-91*
Sheep Year people are elegant and enjoy creature comforts. They are often shy and uncertain, but are accomplished in the arts and have good taste. They are wise, gentle, and caring.

YEAR OF THE MONKEY   *1944-56-68-80-92*
Monkey Year people are extremely inventive, original problem-solvers. They are clever, skillful and flexible, with common sense. They are good at making decisions and want to do things immediately; otherwise they may become discouraged. They have excellent memories and often become famous.

YEAR OF THE COCK   *1945-57-69-81-93*
People born in the Year of the Cock are talented and like to keep busy. They are deep thinkers and try to fulfill any obligation. They are very disappointed if they fail. They always think they are right and usually are. Their emotions swing from high to low. Inwardly they are timid but can be very brave.

YEAR OF THE DOG   *1946-58-70-82-94*
Dog people are deeply loyal, honest, and know how to keep secrets. They are stubborn and care little for wealth, though they always seem to have enough money. They are champions of justice and make good leaders. They are noted for having sharp tongues.

BIRTH MONTH	GEM	FLOWER
January	Garnet	Carnation — *Constancy & Fascination*
February	Amethyst	Violet — *Sincerity*
March	Aquamarine	Jonquil (Daffodil) — *Wisdom*
April	Diamond	Sweet Pea — *Innocence*
May	Emerald	Lily of the Valley — *Love*
June	Pearl	Rose — *Wealth & Caring*
July	Ruby	Larkspur — *Freedom*
August	Peridot	Gladiolus — *Friendship*
September	Sapphire	Aster — *Virtue*
October	Opal	Calendula (Marigold) — *Hope*
November	Topaz	Chrysanthemum — *Fidelity*
December	Turquoise	Poinsettia — *Success*

Index

PARTY ACTIVITIES

All Aboard, 32
Animal Characters Charades, 3
Animal Toss, 15
Announcing Arrivals, 40
Around the Campfire, 46
A Tisket, A Tasket, 9

Back To Your Cages, 58
Baseball Cards, 113
Bert and Ernie Exercises, 23
Bon Voyage, 94
Bop The Pop Can, 58
Broom Relay, 109
Bubble Gum Contest, 113
Buccaneer Buddies, 63

Campfire Tales, 109
Circus Animals, 57
Clowning Around, 57
Coat of Arms, 102
Come To The Carnival, 57
Cookie Letter Bake, 18
Cookie Letter Hunt, 19
Corn Pictures, 4
Count The Beans, 36
Create A House, 68
Cross the Moat, 103

Dead Man's Cove, 63
Dog Catcher, 75
Doggie Biscuits, 74
Dog Race, (Dog Sled Relay), 95
Dress Up, 40

Elf Hats, 150
Enchanted Webs, 27
Enter The Castle, 102

Fairy Crowns and Elf Caps, 150, 152
Farmer In The Dell, 4
Fashion Show, 41
Favorites of Oz, 50
Fetch The Cows, 3
Find The Bone, 75
Find The Cinnamon Bear, 36
Find your Future, 124
Fire Truck Ride, 14
Follow The Yellow Brick Road, 50
Forge A Sword, 102
Fortune Teller, 125

Giddyap, 46
Give The Fairy A Wand, 27
Going To Oz, 50
Great Moments in Sports, 113
Grover's Groovy Shapes, 22
Guess The Letter, 18
Guess The Rhyme, 10
Guess The Rice, 120

Hanakago, 119
Harold Mosell Interview, 112
Harvest Time, 4
Hat Shop, 41
Hayride, 3
Here We Go Round The Mulberry Bush, 9
Hidden Bears, 36
Hobo Face, 108
Hop A Freight, 109
Horoscopes, 125
Hungry Clown, 58

In The Barnyard, 5
Into The Dog House, 74
Into The Dungeon 103
Into The Hoosegow, 45

Jan, Ken, Po, 119
Jan, Ken, Po Relay, 119

Japanese Bath, 120
Jousting, 103

Kermit's Big Time Theater, 23
Kickery, 94
King Of The Hoboes, 108
King Tut, 95
Knighthood Quests, 103

Lantern Maker, 153
Limo Service, 40
Locker Room, 113

Make A Letter, 18
Make A Train, 32
Meet The Wizard, 51
Merlin's Magic, 104
More Letters, 19
Mother Goose Parade, 8
Mubwabwa, 95

Obedience School, 75
Ocha No Kai, 118
Ouija Board, 125

Palm Reading, 124
People Alphabet, 19
Pick A Fortune, 125
Pieces of Eight, 63
Pin The Bow On Teddy, 36
Pin The Mouse On The Clock, 9
Pirates About, 62
Planting Time, 2
Police and Conductor, 108
Pot O' Gold, 27
Promotional Contest, 113

Railroad Ride, 32
Read The Palm, 125
Roundup, 46

Say Hello To Teddy, 36
Search and Rescue, 15
Sherlock Holmes, 22
Slay The Dragon, 103
Snitch The Pie, 109
Space Ride, 80
Stone, Paper, Scissors, 119
Stop The Train, 32
Story Time, 51
Sutter's Mill, 46

Teddy Bear Contest, 36
Tigers Are Out, 58
Time Capsule, 83
Train Time, 32
Treasure Chest, 62
Trivia Quiz, 112
Twenty Years From Now, 126

Umbrella Toss, 57

Village Scene, 70

Westward Ho, 45
What's In The Hobo Bag? 109
What's Missing? 23
Wishing Tree, 118

GAMES

Air Ball, 141
Animal Relay, 138
Animals' Birthday, 129
Arches, 129

Bag of Clothes, 136
Bean Bag Toss, 145
Bingo, 139
Blindman's Bluff, 140
Brownies and Fairies, 133
Bubble Blowing, 145

Call Ball, 136
Cat On The Fence, 77
Charlie Over The Water, 130
Code Messsages, 141
Croquet, 145

Detective, 143
Dog & Bone, 130
Ducks Fly, 133

Favor Exchange, 139

Gossip, 134

Hopping To Boston, 138
Hopscotch, 138
Huckleberry Beanstalk, 133

Lip Reading, 141

Marbles, 145
Marbles in Cups, 142
Mind Teaser, 140
Musical Chairs, 134

Over-Under Relay, 138

Penny Toss, 137
Ping Pong Blow, 141
Pin The Tail On The Donkey, 134
Popcorn Relay, 137
Postcard Puzzles, 138
Puzzles, 129

Raisin Relay, 142
Red Light, Green Light, 139
Red Rover, 135
Rescue Relay, 132
Ring On The String, 130
Ring Toss, 145
Run For Your Supper, 132

Safety Tag, 135
Search, 133
Shoe Scramble, 137
Silver Ball Toss, 135
Simon Says, 134
Snicklefritz, 131
Spoons, 144
Squirrel And Nut, 135
Squirrels In Trees, 142
Sticker Fun, 131
Stunts, 142

The Cheshire Cat Can Make You Grin, 76
Top Spinning, 145
Tricycle Race, 139

Warmer, Warmer, 135
Where Is It?, 141
What's That?, 132
Wheelbarrow Race, 140
Whistle — Soda Cracker, 143
Who Am I?, 143
Who Is Knocking At My Door?, 132
Who's Got The Button?, 130
Who's Missing, 131

CRAFTS

Baker's clay, 148
Boxcar-basket, 149
Bonnet, 151

Collage, 148

Duchess headdress, 150

Elf hat, 150
Engineer's hat, 151

Finger puppets, 148

Hats, 150

Indian headband, 150

Japanese kite, 152

Magnetic puppet show, 148
Megaphone, 150
Merlin's magic hat, 150
Mobiles, 149

Nutshell racers, 148

Paint-a-sheet, 148
Painted cookies, 147
Paper decorations, 152
Paper dolls, 147

Photo adventure, 149
Placemat prints, 149
Pudding pictures, 147

Sand color, 147
Sculpting, 147
Shrinking shapes, 153
Slide art, 149

Sock puppets, 148
Spinners, 153

Tiara or fairy crown, 152
Top hat, 154

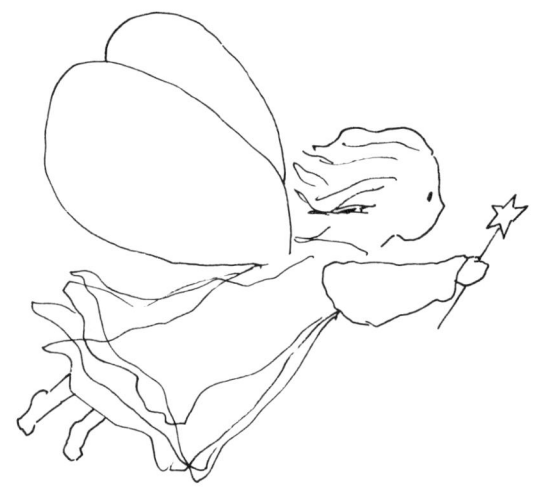

RECIPES

Ashley's Alphabet Cookies, 20

Boardwalk Sandwich, 88
Brownies, 99

Caramel Corn, 99
Circus Soda, 59
Corral Cake, 48
Creamcheese Frosting, 16, 65

Energizer Punch, 115

Fairy Nectar, 29
Fancy Tea Cookies, 42
Five Cup Salad, 91

Gold Doubloon Cookies, 65
Gypsy Goulash, 127

Harvest Bowl, 6
Home Again Applesauce Cake, 96
Hot Fudge Sundaes, 92
Ice Cones, 92
Ice Cream Meows, 77

Merlin's Magic Cake, 106
Milk Shakes, 92

Party Punch, 24
Peanut Butter Bonbons, 71
Peanut Butter Cake, 16

Rainbow Punch, 53
Royal Glue, 71
Rubber Chicken Punch, 110

Sapporo Icebox Squares, 121
S'Mores, 92

Scarecrow Shakes, 6
Star Command Cake, 84

Tangerine Yogurt Dip, 34
Teresa's Pirate Punch, 64

Queen of Hearts Tarts, 11